MW01025912

A NEW MOUNTAIN
TO CLIMB

*Heroes I've Met and the Mountains
They Climb Every Day*

From Wayne Newton

An award winning, legendary entertainer known as "Mr. Las Vegas," actor, and author of Once Before I Go, and Chairman of the USO Celebrity Circle.

What do you call a guy who has such a caring heart he is willing to help at a moment's notice? I call him by his name, Neal McCoy. To say Neal is a giver, is an understatement. He is not only the ultimate entertainer with boundless energy and stunning audience rapport, he is a humanitarian in the most perfect sense of the word. I have asked Neal to join our USO tours many times for many reasons: He is a genuine joy to be around; he's the consummate professional in all situations (even in the most remote bombed out hangar

with no sound system); and, Neal *always* connects –
that's it pure and simple.

Whether entertaining our troops with his music,
charming an audience with his quirky humor, meeting
the President or a child backstage, Neal can make anyone's day. What makes him even more endearing is that
he would never think of himself as especially talented
or unique, yet he is. In fact, there is no one better in
the business at engaging and entertaining an audience.
Congratulations on the book, Neal! Like you, its message of joy and hope will be felt long after the last page
is read.

From Nolan Ryan

*An 8 time Major League All-Star pitcher named to Base-
ball's Hall of Fame in 1999. Holds records for career strike-
outs (5,714), and no-hitters (7). Team President and Owner
of Texas Rangers Baseball team. Author of Nolan Ryan's
Pitcher's Bible, Throwing Heat, and Miracle Man.*

I met Neal several years ago and we became instant
friends. I enjoy his easy-going approach to life. I admire
his music, his home-spun sense of humor, and his great
gift to entertain folks. The man has more life-time fans
than anyone I know.

I once commented that one of the beautiful things
about baseball is that every once in a while you come
into a situation where you want, and where you have
to, reach down and prove something. The same is true
about the people whose stories are included in Neal's

book, *A New Mountain to Climb*. These are stories of real-life people who have to "reach down and prove something" every day. This tenacity makes us human. Now others will see the "real" McCoy, the one I know – the one who has a heart as big as Texas.

From Tommy Franks, General (Ret)

Retired General for the United States Army, former Commander of United States Central Command overseeing United States armed forces operations in 27 countries including Middle East, led invasion of Afghanistan and Iraq, author of American Soldier.

Neal McCoy is an American treasure. There is absolutely no pretense in this country gentleman who hails from Jacksonville, Texas. He can make you laugh one moment and be serious as a Sunday sermon the next. He is everything good our country stands for: a caring artist who sacrifices time, comfort, and safety to enter some of the most dangerous parts of the world just to bring a little enjoyment to our brave men in uniform. I have seen his heart and it bleeds red, white, and blue. I am honored to be a subject in this book on mountains and those who climb them. However, in my opinion, it takes men like Neal McCoy to point the way toward the heights. Neal, you made a difference by providing a glimpse of home and sharing your music with countless service men whose names you will never know. One you do know is – me. My heartfelt thanks to you for being you.

From Bill Mayne

Music industry veteran, President of the Academy of Country Music, Executive Director of Country Radio Broadcasters, owner of Mayne Street Consulting, Nashville.

When I signed on to work with Neal on his independent record label (903 Music) I was familiar with his career from an industry viewpoint, but didn't know the man, his vision, or his passion. What I learned about Neal changed my perspective on him as an entertainer, artist, and human being. I have since used Neal as a glowing example of career vision and work ethic to young developing artists.

Of all the many great artists I have been blessed to work with, Neal has one of the most focused views of who he is – he knows both his strengths and weaknesses. His sole purpose as a performer is to give the audience exactly what they want and he leaves the stage with them wanting more of it. He completely checks his ego and artistic desires and defers to satisfy those people in the seats.

He is the only artist I know who goes onstage every night without a "set" list. In laymen's terms, that means he completely adlibs every show and "custom fits" the songs to the audience in attendance – each and every night. If you see him perform in Dallas then fly to see him in Pittsburg the next night, you will see two vastly different shows. He is the supreme "reader of the room," quickly sizing up each audience and catering to their needs and desires. In business terms, this is called "customer focus" and Neal McCoy delivers for his customers, not himself. His satisfaction comes from pleasing others. He is a giver.

Neal has tireless energy. He uses one of his weaknesses, (his need to continually be doing something), to his advantage. This is where his work ethic kicks into high gear and is in a state of perpetual motion. He is always working to improve his performance: better songs, better band, bigger, bolder moves or routines, better staging, better sound, better PR, promotion. Neal is always striving for the way to do it bigger, better, newer, different; never satisfied with status quo!

Neal has channeled this energy not only into his business, but into his community, and for the greater good. He gives back through the East Texas Angel Network he and Melinda founded. He has volunteered for countless USO Tours, and is willing to help other charitable organizations when asked. It was no surprise when Neal was recognized by both the Academy of Country Music and the Country Radio Broadcasters. He received the Humanitarian Award from both organizations who recognize artists for extraordinary humanitarian efforts.

Finally, Neal has the right attitude to achieve anything. He always has that beaming smile, sense of humor, and a good word. Congratulations on the book, Neal – so proud to know you!

From Karl Malone

2010 Inductee Basketball Hall of Fame, Power forward with records in defensive rebounds and free throws (referred to as the best power forward ever), number retired by Utah Jazz (#32), Member of 'Dream Team' Olympic Gold Medal teams in 1992 and 1996, voted one of the top 50 players to ever play in the NBA.

Neal McCoy is the friend everyone wishes they had - the guy who will tell you what you *need* to hear, not always what you want to hear. From our first meeting, I could tell we would be connected for a lifetime. We can talk for hours, laugh and cut up, or just sit and say nothing. My country roots run deep and Neal and I connect on a genuine level. I respect his commitment to his music and the dedication to showmanship of the finest quality. In fact, the way he approaches his work as a country music entertainer inspired me to work harder, train smarter, and produce at a greater level personally at my game. However the highest compliment I can give Neal is this. My mama loved the man. She smiled just thinking of him. Thanks for including her story in your book, Neal. I'm so glad you knew her. I am proud to call you friend. Let's go fishing sometime soon!

A NEW **MOUNTAIN** TO CLIMB

A NEW **MOUNTAIN** TO CLIMB

Neal McCoy

HEROES I'VE MET
AND THE MOUNTAINS
THEY CLIMB EVERY DAY

TATE PUBLISHING *& Enterprises*

A New Mountain to Climb
Copyright © 2010 by Neal McCoy. All rights reserved.

No part of this publication may be reproduced, stored in a retrieval system or transmitted in any way by any means, electronic, mechanical, photocopy, recording or otherwise without the prior permission of the author except as provided by USA copyright law.

The opinions expressed by the author are not necessarily those of Tate Publishing, LLC.

Published by Tate Publishing & Enterprises, LLC
127 E. Trade Center Terrace | Mustang, Oklahoma 73064 USA
1.888.361.9473 | www.tatepublishing.com

Tate Publishing is committed to excellence in the publishing industry. The company reflects the philosophy established by the founders, based on Psalm 68:11,
"The Lord gave the word and great was the company of those who published it."

Book design copyright © 2010 by Tate Publishing, LLC. All rights reserved.
Cover design by Leah LeFlore
Interior design by Blake Brasor

Published in the United States of America

ISBN: 978-1-61739-434-8

Self-Help / Motivational & Inspirational
11.01.11

TABLE OF CONTENTS

INTRODUCTION

Jacksonville, Texas – my home town is smack dab in the middle of what I think is some of the prettiest country Texas offers. We are proud of our great neighborhoods, great schools, and even greater people who are the "salt of the earth." Up highway 69, a little north of Jacksonville, sits Mission Tejas State Park, a part of the Davey Crockett National Forest, which includes Love's Lookout – the highest point around. It isn't quite a mountain, but the closest to one you will find in these parts. It is actually a long, flat-topped hill that goes for nine miles. Come in spring when the dogwoods are blooming and you will fall in love with the view. See it in autumn, with the blazing colors of the trees and you'll never forget it.

Love's Lookout, named for a peach farmer who purchased 600 acres of the land in 1904, rises 240 feet above the forests below and one can look out over the horizon and it seems to go on forever. It is "our" east Texas "mountain" and I love mountains. At times, miles covered in a tour bus can get monotonous, but anytime we drive through the mountains of Tennessee, Colorado, West Virginia or California, and the great ones of the North East, I'm like a little kid at the window, enchanted with their majesty, their beauty.

Something about all mountains intrigues me, whether they rise up from lush green valleys or dry deserts. I wonder how the early pioneers pulled wagons up and over them to settle this great country. These were tough, gritty people who must have had incredible fortitude, strength and courage.

The difficulties we encounter in life have always been compared to mountains that need to be climbed and conquered. I don't believe there is a person alive who hasn't experienced a hard time when their "mountain" looked to be impassable; so huge that you can't go around it, so high that you can't even see the top for the clouds. Maybe your mountain was a broken relationship, divorce, financial ruin, a betrayal, dashed dreams and hopes, physical limitations, the loss of a loved one – we have all been there. When face to face with our own personal mountains, it can take every ounce of courage and determination just to make it through one more day.

This is a book about people who climb life's most difficult mountains. A while back, a song came to my attention and as I recorded "A New Mountain to Climb," I realized I have encountered some extraordinary people. Their true stories have touched me deeply, even changed the way I live my life. Some of the stories are the direct result of a connection to the East Texas Angel Network that my wife, Melinda and I founded in 1995. Our goal was to help families with expenses arising from caring for a child with a life-threat-

ening disease or children dealing with medical emergencies. These parents and wonderful children we are privileged to help, are some of the bravest, most inspiring people I will ever know, and deserve just a little more help as the children face life-saving surgery and recovery. You talk about mountains? What some children have to endure to have one more day of living on this earth will soften the hardest of hearts and make you feel so blessed. Check out the web site where you can learn more about the organization: East Texas Angel Network (www.easttexasangelnetwork.com).

Someone asked me once about my philosophy of entertainment – how do I perform show after show at the highest level possible? For me, there is no other way. I must leave it all out there on the stage, or I feel I have cheated those who honor us by showing up, giving their time and money to see us in concert. It is a matter of integrity for me, so I give everything I've got to see folks having fun, touched by a particular song, thoroughly entertained. I try to connect with every person in the audience so that when they leave, they feel like they have just spent time with a friend and it went way too fast.

Likewise, I have gained wisdom, insight, energy, purpose, inspiration from time spent in the presence of the people you will meet in the following pages. They too, are giving, or have given their all to scale mountains most of us can't even imagine approaching.

So, here's a book that I hope will bless your heart. Hope – isn't that a great word? It is the single most important commodity in the midst of any crisis. How empty and joyless life would be if all hope was gone. Somehow, someway the people whose stories you are about to read, manage to find hope alive every day. After climbing mountain after mountain, they get up only to face "A New Mountain to Climb." They are my heroes.

~ Neal

"For every mountain, there is a miracle."
—Robert H. Schuller

A MOUNTAIN CLIMBING EXPERT

Shirley Malone Jackson

"I've learned that everyone wants to live on top of the mountain, but all the happiness and growth occurs while you're climbing it."

—*Anonymous*

You wouldn't think we would have many alligator sightings here in East Texas, but it turns out, there have been a few lately. After determining I did not want to go looking for one, I did a little reading on the female alligator's care for her young. First, the mother has no help – she is a single parent and a fierce protector of her young even before birth. She sits nearby, ready to attack any threat to her eggs. The powerfully built body reacts lightning fast. Her huge jaws and teeth (2000 pounds of crushing force) certainly would deter anything that would dare to approach. Then, at the point that the baby alligators need to learn to swim, the mama alligator's ferocious mouth becomes a safe, gentle carrier to transport the hatchlings from the shore to the water. She trains her young for a year or more, making sure they are equipped to survive on their own.

As in nature, some of the greatest mothers have had to provide for, protect, and train their children all alone. The following is a story about a strong yet humble woman. She too, was a fierce protector, mentor, teacher, encourager, but most of all a mother who gave her children roots and wings. She established a firm foundation of faith and confidence. Each child knew they were loved unconditionally. I am privileged to call one of her children a friend, and extremely grateful I knew this great, great lady.

Ten inductees walked across the stage as they were named to the prestigious Naismith Basketball Hall of Fame in August of 2010. Sitting in the audience that evening I leaned in closely to hear the acceptance speech of my friend, Karl Malone. The 14-time named All-Star choked up several times as he thanked his family and his wife, but the tears flowed even more freely near the end when he spoke of his mother, Shirley Malone Jackson. 'Miss Shirley,' as we called her, died seven years earlier to the day, and it was apparent to all, that Malone credited his mom with his success. "I'm here because of her," the 6'9" (arguably the best ever) power-forward declared. I want you to know her too – she was an expert at teaching her children how to climb life's mountains.

~ Neal

"Climb the mountains and get their good tidings."
—John Muir

The funeral was a simple but lovely affair. The El Dorado, Arkansas church was packed with folks having to stand in the back as the service progressed. There were few flowers because the deceased had requested that flowers be given to her while she was alive, not after. She also made it clear that her funeral was not to be long and "dragged-out." Most people were casually dressed, some in jeans and T-shirts and sandals. A pastor made a few comments; her son, NBA great, Karl Malone, gave a touching tribute to his mother. Later, he would say he couldn't even recall what he said, "It was all a blur." Karl had asked me to sing at the funeral and I stepped to the front to sing a tune titled, "When It's Time." The words of the song seemed to fit the occasion and I couldn't help but marvel at the outpouring of love for this woman who had impacted so many in her lifetime. I met Miss Shirley and spent time with her several times through the years because of my friendship with Karl. It was difficult to keep the tears at bay when I thought of this unselfish, loving mom who lived her life totally for others. She would be greatly missed.

Shirley Malone Jackson's death at 66 years of age came as a shock to the family. She had battled diabetes for some time, but no one was prepared for the news on that August day in 2003. Karl was in New York practicing with the USA Olympic Basketball team. He usually spoke to his mother at least once a day, but that morning he had been running late and left his hotel room without checking in with her. When he returned to the room he couldn't reach his mom by phone, so he called his sister who told him their mother was in the hospital. Karl could hear in his sister's voice that it was more serious than she was indicating. Alarmed, he called the hospital and demanded to speak to someone who would give him a thorough update on his mother. A doctor finally broke the news that broke the big guy's heart – she had passed away from a heart attack, only hours before. She was taken suddenly and finally. It was, hands down, the hardest day ever for the "Mail Man," Karl Malone.

The funeral procession followed the hearse and left the church in El Dorado heading toward a cemetery just outside Junction City, Louisiana about thirty minutes away. The line of cars with headlights blazing looked like it was ten miles long. Looking over my shoulder at the cars, I remember thinking; *these are friends, family, neighbors, co-workers, church friends, former employers, NBA basketball stars, wealthy front-office executives, and people from every walk of life showing respect for a wonderful woman who didn't make it past the eighth grade.*

I thought of her life. I wondered if there were times in Shirley's life when the responsibilities seemed overwhelming and the challenges of raising a large family too hard to bear. And now, like a play on life's stage, each act led up to this moment in time, a final earthly scene when all who knew her, as the Bible says, were "rising up to call her blessed."

Most of the residents around the rural area near Junction City, Louisiana where Shirley grew up, farmed some while holding down other jobs. The family kept a cow or two, some chickens, and a few hogs. Shirley grew up knowing how to work hard, she had to. After excelling in school and proving to be a stand-out basketball player herself, she quit school after the eighth grade to help support her family. She worked chopping cotton, milking, working in the fields from dawn to dusk, taking care of younger brothers and sisters.

A young man from the area began a courtship with Shirley and soon after, the children seemed to come almost yearly. It was common practice for Shirley to give birth one day and be expected back to work the next. Summertime in Louisiana is hot, muggy and nearly unbearable. So it was when her youngest son, Karl was born on July 24, 1963 in nearby Bernice, Louisiana. Seven siblings waited for yet another baby to arrive home.

She held several jobs, often more than one at a time. She cleaned homes for local townspeople for years. Later she would work at a lumber company doing a man-sized job as well as any man could do. She was driven to meet the needs of her large brood and always managed to do so. However, there wasn't much left over for anything else.

Her husband walked out on Shirley and the family when Karl, the youngest child, was only four years old. Karl has vague memories of this time but nothing concrete. His father simply was there one day and gone the next. Shirley didn't miss a beat since she had been the main bread-winner anyway. She did not complain about her plight and was not filled with bitterness or regret over the situation. The father would drift in and out of his children's lives from time to time over the years, but he had no significant impact, nor did he help with their support. It was Shirley who pulled in the reins and resolved to be both mother and father to her children.

She could be tough when it was warranted. Karl received his share of spankings and probably "deserved many more," he relates, (and if you know Karl like I do, I'm sure that's true). When her children misbehaved, she would tell them, "I just don't have time for this." And that was that. Discipline was meted out according to the crime. Chores were expected to get done, younger kids were looked after by the older, and every child was taught respect for their elders. She also made it clear that "you were to treat others better than they would even treat you."

Attending church was a major part of the family's life. They attended the New Home Baptist Church and seemed to be there every time the church doors were open. Karl recalls how the family occupied a whole pew by themselves. Also, if there was a revival meetin' at another church, or in a town nearby, Shirley would pack up the kids and off they would go. Karl says with a smile, he was "saved at least two or three times a year." Shirley was a deeply spiritual, sincere woman who made sure that her children heard her pray in good times and in bad. It didn't matter what was going on in her life, she praised the Lord with the same level of love and commitment. Her faith would carry her through the most difficult times and provide her with a "peace that passed all understanding." Giving up was simply never an option and there was no mountain that couldn't be climbed.

Because she personally knew how tough life could be, she was generous to others in need ... almost to a fault. Karl remembers she once had a cow slaughtered and gave half of it to the neighbors who were having a tough time. "Some of us couldn't understand giving so much away, because we needed the beef too," Karl recalled. Shirley was adamant that her children be aware of the plight of those less fortunate. Many times she reminded her children, should they ever acquire financial wealth, they would be obligated to bless others. She never was impressed with money, people who had money, or many of the things money could buy.

Karl, like his brothers, learned to hunt, fish, and play basketball, sort of in that order. At an early age he was shooting squirrels, skinning them, slaughtering hogs (sometimes after riding them just for fun), wringing the necks of chickens and helping feed the family.

He also loved to fish and so did his mom. Every chance she had she grabbed a pole and would be happy sitting along the creek bed for hours. Later in life, when she went fishing, she would say she was "going to work." That was always happy work for this mom who had little real free-time.

Her time in the kitchen spent cooking for her family yielded some larrupin' good stuff. Just ask Karl about his mom's banana pudding, biscuits and gravy, squirrel mulligan stew, fried chicken, and sweet potato pie. To this day he misses the taste of collard greens and fried okra.

Shirley Malone Jackson had an infectious laugh and quick sense of humor. She loved to tell jokes and funny stories to anyone who would listen. She would repeat the stories of cantankerous family members and colorful characters from around Junction City. Her children loved to hear their Mama laugh. She enjoyed the company of many loyal friends and they enjoyed the relationship with her. Her advice was simple but exact, "You be somebody, that when people see you comin,' they be glad to see ya!"

Basketball would come easy to Karl; in spite of the fact the family couldn't even afford a mounted rim for a long time. The earliest memory of practicing basketball for Karl was a sentimental one of his mother fashioning a hoop with her outstretched arms. He would practice throwing the ball through her self-made basket, until her face, arms and chest would be red from being hit with the ball. He had a knack for the game and she knew it from the beginning. She loved to say, "Anybody tell you, you can't do somethin' - show 'em how many ways you can do it!"

The family lived in and around the Mount Sinai area and Karl attended school at Summerfield. Mount Sinai sat a good twenty-five miles from any town of size. During the late 1970's, when Karl was in high school, Summerfield boasted around 260 students from Pre-Kindergarten through the 12th grade. The racial make-up of the school was pretty evenly split between white and black students. The rural setting did not keep crowds from jamming the high school gym for basketball games, especially when Karl Malone was playing. The Rebels of Summerfield High found a star in Karl Malone and he was quickly gaining notice from college scouts. When Louisiana Tech in Ruston, Louisiana offered Karl a scholarship to play basketball, Shirley was extremely proud and sent Karl away to play for the Bulldogs with a promise to make it down to see as many games as possible. He averaged around 20 points and 10 rebounds per game while at La Tech. While there he would begin to earn the nickname he would carry throughout his career: *The Mail Man* – so given, because he delivered on time, every time. His chiseled, 6' 9," 260 pound body, along with his outstanding work ethic and commitment to training, became legendary. The Utah Jazz drafted him in 1985 and the rest, as they say, is history.

Karl admits freely he was not perfect and made some choices as a young man that he regrets very much. His mom, like any good mom, voiced her disappointment and was quick to let him know that every choice in life has consequences, good or bad.

She was also equally quick to tell him how proud she was of him when he deserved it. She would later add, "Of course, I'm proud of Karl, but I am proud of all my children." She made sure her children never felt she favored Karl because of his huge success.

Through out Karl's stellar career in Utah, Shirley was court side often. She spent weeks at a time visiting Karl, his wife, Kay and their children in Utah, but would always return to her roots in Arkansas and Louisiana. About the only thing she truly wanted was to someday have a little house, (somewhere back home) with a white picket fence around it. A couple of years before she passed away, Karl bought the house of Shirley's dreams in El Dorado, Arkansas. Karl told me he had never seen his mom happier than she was during the last two years of her life. She made sure her children understood that "when my time comes, I don't want no wires and machines keepin' me alive. Just let me go." Of course no one believed "her time" would come so quickly.

The cemetery where Shirley is buried sits beside the small church, New Home Baptist Church, where the family attended for so many years in Junction City. Her grave stone included the usual birth and death dates along side a picture of her fishing. A simple phrase signified she was, 'Gone but not Forgotten' and under Shirley's picture, the mention of her favorite pastime. The inscription reads, 'Gone Fishin.' Karl had stocked a pond on property he purchased near El Dorado. Mother and son enjoyed many happy hours there together talking, fishing. After her death it was just too painful to revisit the fishing spot without her; Karl plans to place the property up for sale.

The winding caravan of cars parked along the gravel road entrance and along every dirt road within the small cemetery. Mourners made their way toward the funeral home canopy spread over the newly dug grave where Shirley would be laid to rest. Remarks were made, a prayer was offered while you could hear family members softly sobbing, then most of us walked slowly away with a thousand memories floating through our minds of this dear, sweet mom. A few family members lingered under the funeral home canopy that shielded them from the blazing sun. It was hot, but Karl remembers a cool, pleasant breeze blowing across the casket flowers and cemetery grass. His mother would have enjoyed such a beautiful day.

The most comforting thought to those who grieve a departed loved one is to know that there is nothing left unsaid, unresolved, or unforgiven. Shirley Jackson Malone knew she was valued and loved and freely expressed her love and pride for her children and others every day. As I walked sadly away from the cemetery with my wife, I recalled part of an old poem about the "hand that rocks the cradle." A sudden spark of joy overshadowed my sadness as we exited the cemetery. "Miss Shirley, you were the hand that rocked the cradle and also the hand that ruled the world. You ruled my heart and so many others. We will see you in the mornin.'"

Blessings on the hand of women!
Fathers, sons, and daughters cry,
And the sacred song is mingled
With the worship in the sky—
Mingles where no tempest darkens,
Rainbows evermore are hurled;
For the hand that rocks the cradle
Is the hand that rules the world.

—Wm. R. Wallace

I met Karl Malone by accident back in 1994 and we became fast friends. Who knew that this famous basketball player loved trucks, tractor pulls, professional wrestling, and 'surprise, surprise'… country music? After finding out where he was from, that made a little more sense. When I was asked to be introduced to him, he turned from where he was seated and said, "Well, Neal McCoy!" He knew me and my music. He has been gracious to me and my family and generous to our foundation, the East Texas Angel Network. Karl, his great children and lovely wife, Kay, have given me and my family many treasured memories. You learn from everyone you meet, and my friendship with Karl Malone has taught me many things. I observed his hard work, the push to excel and become the best at what he did. That is what I admired most — absolutely no one was going to outwork him. He would be prepared to show up for every game. He inspired me to work hard to be the best I could be.

He is a giant of a man, but more impressive is Karl's big heart. I have witnessed his generosity on several occasions.

On the day of the Hall of Fame induction, at an earlier press conference/luncheon, Karl was awarded a jacket from the committee (the one with the emblazoned crest naming him a Hall of Famer.) The jacket, for some reason, was many sizes too small; he even mentioned that it was probably too small for his 12 year old daughter! Then, he pulled a real Karl Malone move. After admiring it for a while, as he left the press conference, he handed the jacket to a kid in the auditorium who was sitting in a wheelchair. Karl knew if he kept it he would probably take it out and look at it every now and then, but, "I knew the kid would probably treasure it forever," he said later.

Where did that come from? I knew the answer.

Somewhere out there, above the clouds, Shirley Malone Jackson smiled and said, "Now, that's my boy."

~ Neal

"Faith moves mountains, but you have to keep pushing while you are praying."

—Mason Cooley

"I learn something every time I go into the mountains."

—Michael Kennedy

THE MAN IS THE MOUNTAIN

Tommy Franks, General (Ret)

"To be a mountain, you must climb alone."

—William Stafford

First time I met him I was struck by what a big guy he is – a commanding presence. His face was rugged; lined with time and experience. He gave me his full attention when we were introduced. We shook hands and I still remember his strong grip. He was a hero in my eyes then and now. I would soon discover, this "soldier's soldier" was also a man with a great sense of humor and big heart.

You get a glimpse into a man's soul when they are entrusted with something important. General Tommy Franks assumed Command of the United States Central Command in July of 2000. In that position he had responsibility of 25 countries in east Africa, the Middle East (Afghanistan and Pakistan). He was in leadership there when the September 11th New York terrorist attacks came. He then planned and executed Operation Enduring

Freedom, which removed the Taliban and al Qaeda from Afghanistan.

The purpose of this book was to highlight special people I have met. I couldn't leave out this extraordinary American. He is larger than life to me and I am proud to call him a friend. Men sometimes are no match for the mountains they are asked to climb. Not in this case. He is every bit the man to match any mountain. On second thought, he is the mountain.

~ Neal

"If I have someone who believes in me, I can move mountains."

—Diana Ross

I was on a flight from Columbus, Ohio to Dallas on the morning of September 11, 2001. About an hour into the flight, the pilot suddenly announced over the loud-speaker that we were landing in Little Rock, Arkansas. My first thought was, "Wow, did I get on the right plane? We were supposed to be headed to Dallas." Then in just a moment or two, the pilot again broke in to inform us that there had been a probable terrorist attack in New York City and he had been instructed to land the plane as soon as possible (the first tower at the World Trade Center had been hit). The closest airport to land was the Little Rock airport.

We were in a state of disbelief, and unable to get further information until the plane landed. Upon arrival, I checked my phone, only to see that I had about ten messages about the first tower being hit by an airplane. Everyone in my family and camp were wondering about my whereabouts since the plane that flew into the tower had left approximately the same time my flight left in Ohio, and both were American Airlines planes. They had heard that all planes were being grounded and they were hoping I was on one of them, and if so, they were concerned about where I had landed. As we were walking through the airport, we stopped to watch television monitors and learned the second tower was also hit.

I'll never forget watching people in the airport. They were speaking quietly to each other, stunned, and glued to the television monitors; many in tears. I spoke to my wife as soon as I could and learned further details. It was a surreal experience seeing so many planes landing in the airport. I remembered a buddy who worked with us who was visiting in Hot Springs. We gave him a call and he offered to pick me up and transport me home to Longview, or there is no telling how long I would have been there. Every rental car available was quickly snatched up.

Everyone would remember where they were on one of the darkest days in America's history. Like the rest of the nation, I wept and prayed then, again like most of us, I got angry. I was glad when President Bush said the attack would not go unanswered.

Wayne Newton called me in the latter part of September (before the invasion of Afghanistan) and I was intrigued and interested in his offer. Wayne had taken over as head of the celebrity circle, organizing the USO Tours. Bob Hope had passed the baton on to him, and Wayne was getting a crew together for a tour to Bosnia, Italy and Hungary in November. He invited me to come along. I quickly said, yes, and looked forward to the tour.

There were probably a hundred people who made up the group that participated in that Thanksgiving USO tour to Bosnia. Besides me and Wayne, entertainers Ruth Pointer, Shaggy, Rob Schneider, Jessica Simpson, Bo Derek, Chas Edelstein to name a few, joined the tour along with others. We had a wonderful time and I was grateful for the experience.

We had only been home from that trip for three days when Wayne called again. His demeanor was strangely guarded and solemn this time. He asked me if I could return his call on a land line instead of my cell phone. As soon as I could, I called him back. He informed me that he had been contacted by our state department who requested a tour but he could give me few details. The tour would be at Christmas and I secretly guessed the possible destination. I knew our military forces had recently invaded Afghanistan. I wanted to participate, but this time it would be a little more dangerous, and I would not be able to provide details for my family. Wayne said the boys we would entertain were "in the sandbox" and had been there a little while and could use a little piece of home. I assumed that was some sort of code for meaning out in the field. I told Wayne that I would discuss the invitation with my wife and let him know. After all, this was my first invitation into a war zone.

My wife had concerns, but in the end, she knew I wanted to go and finally agreed to my participation in this very "hush-hush" USO Christmas tour. We all met up in DC. It was a small group this time made up of Wayne, me, comedian Drew Carey, and two Dallas Cowboys cheerleaders, Julie Holman and Melissa Gutierrez. Wayne brought along a key board guy, a drummer with a snare drum, and a guitar player. We were told there would not be much available in the way of sound equipment or stage set up. It was to be a quick in and out thing.

We flew on a military plane from Washington Dulles into Kuwait on or around December 21st. The air was warm and humid as we stepped from the plane to be transported for a very short night in a hotel. We got an early start the next morning. We had a great day visiting and encouraging our soldiers in Kuwait. Then, later that night we were escorted to a nearby hanger. We still had not been told specifically, for our own safety, where we were going or whom we would be entertaining. We soon found out that the soldiers we would entertain had been fighting, maneuvering, and living in the desert and mountains for some 40 to 45 days.

A big Suburban pulled up and all eyes fastened on the man who crawled out from the back seat. General Tommy Franks is a big man with a John Wayne type physique. He strode confidently into the hangar and immediately shook hands with each of us as we were introduced to him. He was warm, welcoming, and appreciative. "Thank you for coming over to see our soldiers. It is an honor to meet you." An honor to meet us? We were awe struck by this man who was in command of the nation's war efforts.

It was then we were informed we were headed into Afghanistan. On the plane ride over to Camp Rhino near Kandahar Airport the General was talkative, gracious, and endearing. He told me he was a long time fan and I suppose we connected because we both hail from Texas. We hit it off immediately.

Camp Rhino (closed shortly after we had been there) sat in the desert, thirty five miles south of Kandahar. The airport was built by a rich Arab sheik who used it sparingly for hunting trips. Frequent dust storms and the rugged nearby mountains made landing difficult at times.

After landing in complete darkness, we were escorted into a dark hangar. Once inside, someone flipped on a generator and we were astounded by the sight of 600 soldiers standing at parade rest in a tight U-shaped formation.

My heart was touched by the sight of these dirty, tired, young men who hadn't showered in weeks, honoring us as they stood in appreciation. To deafening applause, General Franks walked to a microphone and spoke to them for a few moments and then with a tiny PA system we entertained them for about an hour and then got to walk around and meet some of the bravest young men I will ever meet. I approached one and said, "Pretty tired, huh?" He answered, "Yes, sir, it's been a pretty tough go. If you don't mind, may I sit down for a while?" I quickly responded, "Absolutely, young man," (as if I had the proper authority to do so).

One Navy Seabee stood nearby and I admired the camouflage shirt he wore where the name McCoy was proudly displayed (I never learned his first name). A few moments later McCoy found me and offered me his shirt. He insisted I take it, saying he had received permission from a superior to give it to me as a gift. (I still have the shirt hangin' in the closet – I never washed it and I actually wear it now and then and remember the young McCoy – I sure hope he made it back safely).

We loaded back into the plane and headed for Kandahar airport. We were all talking about the experience, the reception, and how encouraged we were to meet such fine young men. General Franks was again talkative and complimentary of the job we did for the soldiers. He wore a 45 caliber pistol strapped to his side at all times, even in the airplane. The General's wife, Cathy, accompanied us as well. It was clear that the General had the unwavering support of his wife and she was charming and gracious to all.

I had watched the news and knew we had just bombed the Kandahar airport and I was hoping it was in good enough shape to land. It was dark when we landed and the pilot was using infrared instrument readings. The door of the plane opened and I noticed again how the air outside was hot and humid. Even at 3 a.m. it was probably 90 degrees. (It didn't ever get much cooler.) Absolutely no light could be seen as we exited the airplane. Soldiers with night-vision goggles escorted us to vehicles that would transport us to the hangar. The darkness was so intense that we could only hear the motors running on the vehicles awaiting us that sat only twenty feet away. Literally you couldn't see the hand in front of your face.

Once inside the hangar we saw sheets covering bombed out windows and a concrete floor. And there again were more soldiers, but this time they were crouched in close to a makeshift stage area, actually just an open space on the concrete floor only a foot or two from where we would perform. Again, even though tired and battle-worn, the soldiers gave us a rousing welcome. It was sobering to see them sitting there smiling, swaying to the music, some so dirty that the only clean spot on their faces was the outline of where their goggles had been.

I had joked with the General on the trip over, "So, being the General and Commander of these men, you could ask them to do anything, and they would have to do it – right?"

"Well, technically, I guess that is right," General Franks answered.

I had forgotten the statement until General Franks mentioned it during the program that evening. "Soldiers, Neal McCoy here wanted me to order you to do something... to prove my authority that would show him you guys would follow any orders from me."

I thought, "*Oh, no, these guys are gonna hate me – he's gonna ask them to drop and give him fifty push-ups or something...*"

But, he continued, "So, here's what I want you to do. I want you to turn to the soldiers beside you and give them a big hug."

Well, a lump came to my throat and I nearly cried at the sight of these men hugging each other and expressing real affection for their brothers-in-arms." Right then and there I decided General Franks was a true genius.

We didn't get to finish the program that evening. Drew Carey was in the middle of his routine when the program was halted and we were scurried out of the hangar. We never knew the nature of the emergency, only that it was necessary the hangar be cleared as soon as possible and that the USO troupe get back in the air.

Since the USO Tours mentioned above I have had the privilege of being with General Franks on several other occasions. I guess old country boys from Texas just naturally get along. I discovered he has a great sense of humor, loves to joke around – he is a genuinely happy person. Here's another thing you may not know about General Franks. He loves to sing – yep, he can belt out quite a few country tunes. In fact, he loves Charley Pride (also a long time Texas resident) and I enjoyed introducing the General to Charley a few years ago in Dallas at Charley's home. It was during the Cotton Bowl on New Years Eve. I don't know who was more excited, the General or Charley. Anyway, the General will rear back and start singing, "Kiss An Angel Good Mornin" just anytime (a song Charley made famous).

We have remained friends and through the years I have gained more insight into the priorities and passions of this real American hero. General Franks makes mention in his book, *American Soldier*, of his father, Ray Franks, whom he respected and admired very much.

He learned some powerful and meaningful lessons from his father who made sure young Tommy knew there were consequences for every decision. Even a visit to McAlester State Prison in Oklahoma, as a young boy scout, would resonate with him for the rest of his life. Tommy Franks was taught to do his best, (whatever the work), appreciate the value of a dollar, and to honor his word above all.

Like most of us, there were some rough spots along the way to adulthood for the young Franks as he sought direction and a career. The family relocated from Oklahoma to Midland, Texas, when Tommy was in the fifth grade. He played football through high school, enjoyed scooters, then cars and of course, girls. He enrolled at the University of Texas in Austin, but his party life and lack of serious study landed him on academic probation. He was aware of the war in Vietnam and decided after a night of heavy drinking that being a soldier sounded pretty good. On the morning of August 20, 1965, Tommy Franks was the first person through the door at the Austin Army recruiting station. The Army was about to remake a kid and offer him the opportunities of a lifetime.

The Army became a perfect fit for Tommy. He needed the discipline, the order, the earned respect given when a task or exercise was accomplished. In October of 1967, Tommy received orders to report for a flight to Vietnam to begin a stint. His father had a word of advice for his son at the Greyhound Bus Station just before heading out. With tears in his eyes, Tommy's dad said,

"Well, make 'em a hand, son."

You see, to Ray Franks, a "hand" was the most valuable kind of man. Ray had worked around oil fields, garages, cotton fields and drilling rigs all of his life. A good "hand" was the man who pulled his own load, earned his daily wage, and did his job to the best of his ability.

"I'll sure try, Dad," was the young Franks' answer. Ray Franks passed away in 1986 and it was one of the most difficult days for the General who still wishes he had access to his dad's insight, wisdom and fellowship.

From Vietnam to Commander in Chief of the United States Central Command during Operation Iraqi Freedom, Tommy Franks has made America "a hand." That was my persisting thought as I watched him cross the stage at his retirement ceremony in July of 2003. He had called and asked if I would be a part of the ceremony that would mark his retirement. He especially loved a song that I had recorded, titled, "I'm

Your Biggest Fan." General Franks had heard me sing the song numerous times and he requested that I sing the song during the farewell event. He would be handing over command to General John Abizaid at McDill Air Force Base in Tampa, Florida. The ceremony was a big "to-do" covered by all news networks and then Secretary of Defense, Donald Rumsfield was the featured speaker.

Secretary Rumsfield began to laud General Franks and his history-making decisions and victories. As he spoke, my mind went back to the night I sang for some tired, dirty marines, short on rest, but full of appreciation. I recalled the one in particular who had asked permission to sit down for just a moment. Here was General Franks getting ready to enter retirement, but, for the life of me, I couldn't see him just sitting down and taking it easy.

Rumsfield was saying some wonderful things about the General but my thoughts were targeted on the things that most people might never know about the man. I thought, *most of them don't realize that on September 7ᵗʰ (four days before the attacks of September 11ᵗʰ) General Franks spoke of possible terrorism within our country's borders.* He was speaking to the CENTCOM intelligence staff when a young sergeant asked, "General, what keeps you up at night?"

For a moment the General paused then spoke, "A terrorist attack against the World Trade Center in New York – that's what keeps me awake at night."

The General recounts in his book how the audience became stone-quiet as he continued, "If terrorists were to strike a major blow against us, I fear the specter of the nation's military operating as combatants within our borders for the first time since the 1860's," he said, then continued. "So, the thing that keeps me awake at night, Sergeant is the possible use of armed forces against American citizens. We do our job well, but we're trained to fight foreign enemies. We're not police officers, sheriffs, or the FBI. If we were ever required to act in that capacity during a major emergency like an attack on the World Trade Center, the effect on America could be devastating. Martial law would not sit well in a free and open society." Imagine his shock on September 11th when the General heard his random analogy had become a prophetic and tragic reality.

Secretary Rumsfeld finished his comments by introducing General Franks to the audience who then walked to the podium while the audience stood and cheered. He first expressed gratefulness for the support of the Secretary and President. Then, he tenderly directed comments to his wife, Cathy – thanking her for her years of service to the nation. He clearly knew his achievements would not have been possible if not for her presence in his life. Then he discussed the changing political landscape of our country and how global war on terrorism would be on-going because our "way of life" is at stake. He left the stage and my heart soared with pride. This man who had known presidents, war lords, generals, sheiks, and kings was a man I could call a "friend."

The general stays busy now speaking and lecturing around the country and of course, always stands ready in an advisory capacity. He and Cathy spend time in Texas, Florida and on their spread in Oklahoma. A few years ago I asked the general to do the intro (lead-in) for a song we were recording, titled, *The Last of a Dying Breed*. I knew the song would be meaningful to the General because of the special relationship he had with his father and the song was a salute to men just like Ray Franks. General Franks wrote an incredibly moving lead-in and the song remains a crowd favorite to this day. To me, the song seems to fit General Franks as well. There simply will never be anyone like him ever again. With all my heart, I thank him, not only for serving our country but for being the example of a die-hard, unabashed patriot who would saddle up again should his country come calling.

Since the theme of this book focuses on mountains, I tried to find a title for this chapter that was suitable for General Franks and I came to the realization that he IS the mountain. Then, I ran across this poem written long ago by William Stafford. The words of the poem offer a perfect description of a man who deserves every ounce of his nation's admiration and respect.

To be a mountain you have to climb alone
and accept all that rain and snow. You have to look
far away, when evening comes. If a forest
grows, you care; you stand there leaning against
the wind, waiting for someone with faith enough
to ask you to move. Great stones will tumble
against each other and gouge your sides. A storm
will live somewhere in your canyons hoarding its lightning.

If you are lucky, people will give you a dignified
name and bring crowds to admire how sturdy you are,
how long you can hold still for the camera. And some time,
they say, if you last long enough you will hear God;
a voice will roll down from the sky and all your patience
will be rewarded. The whole world will hear it: "Well done."

Indeed, General Franks – all of America echoes that senti-
ment. You are the mountain. Well done, soldier, well done!

~ Neal

"The mountains were his masters. They rimmed in life. They were the cup of reality, beyond growth, beyond struggle and death. They were his absolute unity in the midst of eternal change."

—Thomas Wolfe

"Mountains are earth's undecaying monuments."

—Nathaniel Hawthorne

FISHING ON THE MOUNTAIN

Matthew Barney

*"It's wonderful to climb the liquid mountains of the sky.
Behind me and before me is God and I have no fears."*
—Helen Keller

Some people love to fish for the fish, then, some people just love fishing. Matt Barney loved fishing – he didn't even like the taste of fish. In fact, when I think of Matt, that is how I picture him; sitting in a boat, or propped up on a bank somewhere, fishing pole in hand, and jabbering up a storm with anyone who will listen.

I met Matthew Shem Barney and his family in 1991 when Matt was six years old. He had been diagnosed with cancer the year before. I performed at a fundraiser for Matt in Tombstone, Arizona and we became fast friends. The youngster was full of life and promise. His cancer remained in remission for two years and everyone hoped and prayed that it was gone for good. As it turned out, the cancer returned. Our hearts were broken when we heard Matt had passed away. I wish everyone could have known this loving, vivacious kid who loved to fish.

In his short life, Matt discovered what most of us spend a lifetime learning. What really counts most is time spent with family, expressing love for one another, the power of laughter and fun, and living every day with no regrets. Matt taught us so much about living life to the full, no matter the mountains he had to climb.

Fishing suited Matt Barney and he was good at it. Doug Larson wrote, "If people concentrated on the really important things in life, there'd be a shortage of fishing poles." I know Matt would agree. To him, fishing was a therapeutic joy that could be both calming and exciting. It provided time for building relationships with family, good conversations, and reflection. There was a strength Matt gained from hours of sitting in a boat, surrounded by a beautiful lake. He lives on in a million sweet memories and in the people blessed to know him.

~ Neal

"If you wait for the perfect moment when all is safe and assured, it may never arrive. Mountains will not be climbed, races won, or lasting happiness achieved."

—Maurice Chevalier

Shem and Donna Barney were elated when their son, Matthew was born in April, 1985. Though he was five weeks early, Matt arrived all wiggles and fun from the beginning. At that time the family lived in San Manuel,

Arizona, part of a tri-community area located about 45 miles northeast of Tucson. San Manuel, established in the early '50's to support the copper industry, sits in the San Pedro River Valley area. Most of the town's population of four thousand, worked in the mills, the mines or the smelter operation. The mines would later close, but when Matt arrived in '85, San Manuel was the perfect place to raise an adventurous boy with lots of living to do.

Matt was an inquisitive toddler who inherited a quick wit, sense of humor and a cantankerous nature from his dad, Shem. He most resembled his father, physically as well - big, captivating brown eyes, olive skin, and an abundance of dark brown hair. As he grew older, he told jokes, loved a good practical joke, and squabbled normally with his younger sister, Kimberly Danelle. Matt couldn't pronounce her name correctly so he called her "Kimmy Nell" and it stuck.

Matt had an interest in all things "boy" - athletics, hunting, and he was introduced to fishing at an early age by his grandpa, Marvin Harmon and great-great grandparents, Walt and Juanita Swingle, all now deceased. Other fishing buddies included his friends (Matt adopted them as grandparents), Dan and Mae Boone, as well as uncles, Mike Barney and Steve Harmon. Even sister, Kim and a great-great uncle, C. F, spent time on the lakes with Matt. His favorite place to fish was San Carlos Lake east of Phoenix. Surrounded by desert and low rolling hills, the lake was formed by the Coolidge Dam on the Gila River and actually sits on an Apache Indian Reservation. Matt would fish here for hours at a time, sometimes hauling in more than forty a day (closer to 80 on some days). Funny that Matt caught so many fish, and was always eager to share his catch with others, because, as mentioned, he never liked eating them himself.

In October 1990, when Matt was five years old, a fever and swollen gland in his neck caused the Barneys to schedule an appointment with the doctor. Antibiotics were prescribed and these symptoms faded somewhat only to return again by November. This time however, Matt also had developed an unexplained pronounced limp which further concerned the parents and the doctor. After once more visiting the doctor, the Barneys and Matt were sent home with a stronger round of antibiotics. The doctor also instructed the parents to bring Matt back if there was no improvement within a few days. Donna Shem tells of the events leading up to the doctor's prognosis.

"Matt was not better so we made the trip back to the doctor. Most of our family was in town for the Thanksgiving holiday, but we were focused on finding out what was wrong with our son. For further tests and more thorough examinations, Matt was admitted into the hospital and we anxiously awaited any news about his condition. Then, the very next day, the diagnosis was reported and the grim news hit us like a ton of bricks. A bone scan revealed Matt's pronounced limp was the result of cancer on the bone in his leg. Matt had Stage IV Nueroblastoma, a childhood cancer that begins on the adrenal gland positioned on the kidney."

Stage IV cancer – that's what Matt had, but what did that mean? In layman's terms, the stages of cancer describe how much the cancer has spread, whether it has invaded nearby organs or lymph nodes, and if it has spread to any distant organs. Of Stages I through IV, Stage IV is the most serious. The Barneys were stunned.

The worst news you usually hear about your five year old is that they misbehaved in Sunday School; they called another kid a name, or were being punished for refusing to go to bed or eat their vegetables. To say this was bad news for Donna and Shem Barney and their friends and family is a great understatement. It was beyond bad, it is a parent's worst nightmare. The mind begins a process of mental gymnastics to help people cope with this kind of news:

There has to be a mistake – doctors make diagnosis mistakes all the time – this can't happen, not to us. Look at him he is perfect. God would not allow this. I will refuse to believe it and if I keep denying it, it will go away. I must maintain unwavering hope... unrealistic, over the top hope. I will not hear or believe any negative reports. I will bargain with God, "Please God, put it on me, not my child. I'll do anything! I beg you, make it go away!" Above all is the overwhelming desire for it to just not be true.

The doctor who first treated Matt suspected cancer all along and suggested hospitalization immediately. Later, Donna Barney credited this doctor with extending her son's life.

Three days later, Shem carried his son into the Pediatric Cancer Center in Tucson because Matt was unable to walk on his own. After initial examinations, doctors told the parents that there was little hope Matt would leave the hospital, his condition was just too advanced. That night, kneeling beside Matt's bed, Shem pleaded, "Heavenly Father, if you need to take Matt, take him, but please, don't let him suffer."

A treatment plan was explained to the parents as Matt lay in his hospital room. It would involve powerful drugs with names difficult to pronounce. During a visit with his Aunt Cindy after the doctors left, suddenly Matt became very agitated, "Aunt Cindy, they want to give me drugs and they told us in school we were not supposed to take drugs!"

Matt's concerns were allayed and he became calm again after the doctor explained these drugs were different – they were "medicines to help you get better."

Two weeks later, against all odds, Matt was released from the hospital and was doing much better, but no one had told Matt why he was sick. How do you tell a five year old that he has a serious illness like cancer? On the trip home from the hospital the family stopped for a red light when a very old, rusty looking car pulled up alongside their car. The rust was so bad that it had eaten holes through the metal in several places on the car. Shem took the opportunity to explain exactly what it was that was making Matt sick.

"Matt, see the rusty car with the spots on it? That is sort of like cancer. If they had taken care of the rust on the car when it first started, it wouldn't have spread like that and caused those holes." He lovingly told Matt that cancer was like that - it could spread in the body like rust on a car, but the doctors were taking care of it by getting Matt the right medicine and treatment. Matt was content with that explanation.

The family's routine changed drastically to accommodate Matt's doctor's visits, his treatment schedule and upcoming surgeries. The enormous medical expenses began to mount and Shem had to work so bills could be paid. At one point the cost for just one of Matt's medications was $2,800 for a 20-day supply. Each time Matt's temperature spiked or an infection was detected, it required a hospital stay in a private room. This cost was not covered by insurance. Then there was the expense of traveling back and forth to the hospital over an hour away.

Donna would not work outside the home during this time in order to be free to make Matt's appointments and be with him during the hospital stays. The time away from Kimberly who was just two and a half years old when Matt was diagnosed, weighed heavily on the Barneys as well. Matt's constant care forced the family to rely on friends and family to help care for their little girl. Grandmas and grandpas, aunts, uncles, cousins, friends and neighbors all rallied around the family to offer support, some providing meals, even cleaning the home in Donna's absence.

The Barneys' hometown of San Manuel took personal interest in Matt and there were many fundraisers planned. The events were sponsored by caring people who genuinely wanted to help the family with travel and hospital expenses. The Barneys were immensely grateful for the outpouring of love.

Once a few weeks after the first hospital stay, while the family was eating dinner, Matt asked his parents if they "knew that people with cancer could die?" Thinking that perhaps Matt had been teased at school about his condition, Shem inquired angrily. Matt answered, "No, Dad, I *am* in kindergarten you know!"

The hospital stays were particularly trying for Matt. He had to receive blood and platelet transfusions quite often. Once returning home from Maryland where Matt had received treatment, a bloody nose caused major concern for the flight crew. The nose-bleed could not be stopped and fearing the worst, paramedics were summoned to await the plane as it landed. He was immediately transported to the hospital for a blood transfusion.

Countless trips were made by car to the University Medical Center in Tucson. Matt and Donna would sometimes see deer along the way. Matt heard that if you hit a deer with your car by accident, you could claim the deer. Already an experienced hunter, Matt began to take along his deer caller and a knife, "just in case," he said. Once they stopped at a spot where Matt had seen a couple of deer. Donna stood by while Matt stepped out into a field with his deer caller in hand. A low hill rose before him as he used the caller. To their surprise, suddenly, a herd of cattle appeared cresting the hill and coming fast toward Matt. He and Donna made a dash for the car, laughing the whole time.

The youngster's sense of humor carried the family through many a trying day. He would joke with the doctors and nurses and had a mischievous giggle that showed up often. Donna recalls, a team of doctors watching while one doctor was pressing around on Matt's stomach asking, "Matt, does this hurt?" "How about here, this hurt?" Finally Matt said, "Doctor, does your face hurt?" He replied, "No, why do you ask?" Matt said "Because it sure is killing me!" The old come-back line had everyone laughing.

The local newspaper printed a series of stories on the Barneys and their challenging journey while battling Matt's cancer. Soon afterwards, a Tucson television station, KGUN 9 TV, thought the story would make for a great human interest feature. Guy Atchley, a distinguished veteran newscaster, came to interview Matt and the family in their home. Matt was acting uncharacteristically shy and hesitant during the interview until Guy rose to retrieve a microphone from across the room. Suddenly, Matt stuck his foot out and tripped Guy who nearly tumbled down completely. Donna recalls, "Thankfully, Mr. Atchley had a sense of humor and laughed at himself while Matt giggled in delight." The newscaster would become a friend of the family, organizing and promoting fundraisers for Matt, providing tickets to the family for events, and keeping in close touch throughout Matt's illness.

The Barney family, including Matt, loved country music so they were excited to learn the band and I were scheduled to entertain for a special fundraiser to be held in Tombstone in late September of 1991. The man organizing the event had read about Matt and happened to book country music stars for such events. I am forever grateful for the opportunity to meet Matt and his family.

I knew right away that Matt and I were going to get along. He was a cut up, just like me. I felt like I had known the family forever. Then, whenever we were playing nearby, the Barneys showed up and Matt and I renewed our friendship.

Matt was scheduled for a bone marrow transplant in San Diego soon after we first met. When I returned to Texas I told my wife, Melinda and mother-in-law, Patsy about this special young man. We had been discussing the possibility of setting up a foundation to help families like the Barneys who were going through challenging times with their kids' illnesses. The East Texas Angel Network was still a ways from being organized but I have always felt that meeting Matt and his family gave me a deeper sense of urgency to help. It would be 1995 before we established the Network.

I asked the Barneys to come out to see us play at Billy Bob's in Fort Worth. The famous country and western night club features live bull riding on the weekends and has a small indoor rodeo arena too. They flew out and we outfitted him and his sister in cute cowboy duds and we had a great time.

Two other events I recall with Matt. I invited Matt and his sister to be part of the video shoot for the song, "Wink," in New Mexico. They were featured in that video that millions viewed. During that visit, Matt had heard I had made a bet with a television show host that if I had a hit song I would cut my hair, which was pretty long at that time. Sure enough, "No Doubt About It" took off. Matt, decided it was time for me to hold up my end of the bargain. Somehow he found some scissors and chased me around threatening to cut my hair to "keep me honest." I finally convinced him I needed all the hair I could grow

Then later, I also invited the whole family out to be a part of one of the first events sponsored by our newly formed East Texas Angel Network. Matt was a trooper and so much fun. Other stars joining us that day included Tracy Byrd, Charley Pride, Ricky Lynn Gregg and I am sure Matt never forgot meeting Karl Malone (the one and only "Mail Man") of the Utah Jazz basketball team. In two months Matt would be gone.

My own son, Swayde, had been born during this period and I would often try to put myself in Shem and Donna's place. It must have been overwhelming at times. We take it for granted, but I have thanked God many times for the health of our children.

Matt was not always the prankster. He had profound and sensitive moments and his family recalls each one. For example, when his Mom would look care worn and tired, Matt would say, "Mom, its okay, don't worry – everything will be fine." She believed it - she had to, there was no other way to make it through. On another occasion he was recuperating for the surgery to remove the tumor from his kidney. It happened to be his mother's birthday and Matt, though in extreme pain, reminded everyone that it was his mom's birthday. He seemed especially excited to see the flowers that his dad had sent to the hospital for his mom.

Inevitably, Matt began to lose his hair from the chemotherapy treatments. He noticed quickly others who were bald or nearly bald. Butch Norton was one of those friends. Matt would say, "Butch, now we look alike, but I'm still better lookin.'" Then there was neighbor, Cip Haro, also challenged in the hair department. "Hey, Cip, I may be bald just like you, but my hair will grow back," Matt quipped. The hair did grow back for a while and then one day Matt asked Cip to give him a buzz haircut.

"Why?" Cip asked.

"Because it's back," Matt replied.

"What's back, Matt?"

"The cancer," Matt said very stoically.

Cip was speechless for a moment, moved by the boy's bravery and demeanor.

Winter came as usual to Arizona in November 1995, bringing mild temperatures averaging around 45 to 50 degrees. The streams through the rocky canyons turned much colder and the Arizona sycamores growing along the water's edge had lost all their blossoms. On Thanksgiving Day Shem Barney, an equipment operator, had to work the evening shift at Freeport-McMoRan Copper & Gold. He returned home around 1 a.m. and as always, immediately checked on the children in their bedrooms. He was surprised to find Matt awake.

"Matt, why are you awake?" Shem asked.

"Dad, I can't sleep. Mom let all these people in and they are keeping me awake," Matt's eyes darted to the corners of the bed.

Shem saw no one else in the room but a sudden, jolting acknowledgement swept through his mind. *The presence of others – those lovingly assigned to transport Matt to heavenly places were there and only visible to Matt.* Shem's heart ached. He knew his son was preparing to cross a grand divide where there would be no pain, no cancer – only light and joy forevermore.

"You want some ice, son?" asked Shem in a whisper. By this time Matt's ravaged body could only tolerate crushed ice.

"Yes," was Matt's response.

Shem turned the blender on to crush the ice and later would recall eerily sensing that those present left the room at least for a time.

The next morning, a Sunday, the ambulance arrived early. Matt was sitting up, strong and talking to the very end. One of the paramedics tried giving Matt oxygen by slipping on an oxygen mask. Matt immediately wrenched it off and threw it down. When Guy Atchley heard that account, the newscaster commented, "Isn't that just like Matt to go out the way he came in, with all the fervency and fire and fight that he could muster?"

Then, he was gone, almost five years to the day when he was first diagnosed with cancer. Grieving family and friends remained in town following the Thanksgiving holiday to attend the funeral. We had tried to keep in touch, checking in with the Barneys off and on, but when I heard the news it was still a shock. We were on the road, but I found a quiet place and prayed for the Barneys, and thanked God I had the privilege of knowing such a brave young man.

Nearly a thousand folks crowded the chapel for the funeral. Guy Atchley was one of the speakers. Guy's comments were touching:

"Matthew stayed with us ten years, half of which were spent fighting cancer. He did not complain about his plight, and he tried not to show his pain, but it was there – constantly. We tend to measure a life in days, weeks, months and years. But there is another way; by its impact. Matt was only a little boy, but his struggle brought us together in faith. Matthew was only a little boy, but his courage gave us hope. Matthew was only a little boy, but he taught us the meaning of love."

A video was shown of Matt through out his brief life; the song that played in the background was our song, "No Doubt About It"; there wasn't a dry eye in the place. Following the service seven year old Kimberly was held aloft by her uncle as she said, "I love you, Matt," then Kimberly and the crowd released several hundred balloons toward the sky in Matt's honor.

Matt was laid to rest at Evergreen Cemetery in Tucson. The family chose a black granite headstone with a picture of Matt etched on it, along with a boat on a lake and the words *Gone Fishing*. The epitaph reads:

Matthew Shem Barney, April 9,

1985 – November 26, 1995

Beloved son, brother and grandson

The Barneys now reside in Safford, Arizona and Shem continues working at the Safford copper facility and Donna is the Senior Human Resources Assistant for the same company. Matt's sister, Kim is now happily married, but still misses the presence of her brother. She writes:

"I was so young that I couldn't understand the seriousness of Matt's illness. As the sibling of a terminally ill child, maturity has revealed to me, that I was never overlooked, it was simply that Matt needed my parents more during those few years. I was well taken care of by family and friends while Matt was in and out of the hospital. I do have some treasured, wonderful memories of times with Matt, things we would do together and I feel connected to him through those memories. I often feel Matt wrapping his arms around me like he did when we were kids, especially when I am going through a challenging time. Matt's passing has given me a better understanding and compassion for what siblings experience when faced with similar circumstances."

Donna Barney tells me that Matt loved collecting rocks. Once while hiking near an old abandoned silver mine, he found some with unusual leaf fossils on them.

He carted them home proudly. After Matt's passing, as stated, the couple relocated to Safford, Arizona. They were doing a final walk through in their new home when Donna and Shem excitedly discovered that their new fireplace was constructed with rocks that looked exactly like the ones Matt had collected. There were leaf fossil imprints all over them. This revelation would be a continual reminder of a dear son. Like the leaves that became permanently attached to ancient stones, so Matthew Barney has left his imprint forever on our hearts.

Most would say that the trip up a mountain is harder than the descent, but in the case of Shem and Donna Barney I'm not sure they would agree. After you struggle with all your might to reach the top of mountain after mountain, a unique despair must set it when you discover there are no more mountains to climb. What then? When you have exhausted every type of treatment available, when the medicine no longer has affect, when the fight to reach the summit of each new mountain for your child is gone – the coming down has to be the hardest time of all. All that is left is the bittersweet walk down the other side without your loved one. Only a mother and father who have been through such an ordeal can understand this special kind of pain and loss. I know Matt's parents and sister would say the same thing: Climbing each mountain for Matt was worthy of the

climb and they would do it all over again. Yep, they would climb every one of those mountains again ... that is love.

I miss Matt Barney. Somewhere he is in perfect health, enjoying a beautiful endless day, and probably doing what he loved most. "Hey, Matt, hope you're fishin' a great lake, buddy."

~ Neal

"Without mountains the air could not be purified, nor the flowing of the rivers sustained."

—John Ruskin

"I just want to do God's will. And he's allowed me to go to the mountain. And I've looked over, and I've seen the promised land! I may not get there with you, but I want you to know tonight that we as a people will get to the promised land."

—Martin Luther King

WHY THIS MOUNTAIN?

Mickey Gilley

"Climbing above all, is a matter of integrity."
—*Gaston Rebufat*

I gotta' be honest. I have a lot of questions for God, someday. I don't understand why some things are allowed to exist in the world like poverty, child abuse, natural disasters, war, and disease. An equal mystery is how terrible things can happen to really good people. I don't understand the cruel twist of fate that would steal away a person's means of enjoyment, talent, or livelihood. Life, as we learn by living it, is just not always fair.

Some mountains don't surprise us; we have seen them coming. The mountain looms in the distance and we can sort of gear up and prepare for the climb because we were expecting it. Others appear out of no-where. We are going our way, then, wham! A mountain so big and daunting drops down before us and blocks out everything else. We are stunned by the enormous prospect of having to climb this mountain that seems overwhelming.

A long-time legend in the music industry was challenged with just such a mountain. He must have posed the question many times: "Why this mountain, and why now?" I admire his fortitude, attitude, and unrelenting grit. Mickey Gilley's mark in the field of music will forever be niched, but he deserves even greater accolades for taking on his mountain. "Don't give up, my friend, you are nearing the top."

~ Neal

"I think when you begin to think of yourself as having achieved something, then there's nothing left for you to work towards. I want to believe that there is a mountain so high that I will spend my entire life striving to reach the top of it."

—Cicely Tyson

It was an injury that shouldn't have happened. On July 5, 2009, country music legend, Mickey Gilley was helping a friend move a piece of furniture out of a house in Branson, Missouri. The love seat only weighed about forty pounds. Carrying his end of the small couch, Mickey walked backwards out the door onto the porch then tripped off a ledge no more than 18 or 20 inches high. He landed hard on his neck and the fall rendered him immediately unconscious. He was rushed to the hospital in nearby Springfield, Missouri and the news was not good. He had suffered a serious spinal injury that damaged the cervical (neck area) and in particular, the C4, 5, 6 and part of the C7 vertebrae. Mickey, unconscious for two days in intensive care, awoke to hear that he was paralyzed from the neck down. Doctors assured him feeling in his legs would return and that possibly he may eventually have a full recovery. But it was the injuries to the #6 and #7 vertebrae that could seriously affect the future of a talented man who lived for the music he made.

Anyone who has seen Mickey Gilley perform knows the magic he created at the keyboard – magic we may or may not ever see again. Because of the injury specific to those particular vertebrae, those talented fingers could be affected long-term or possibly forever. If you ask Mickey about it, he will say, "It's just a matter of time." I hope so, buddy, I really hope so.

I don't remember where I was when I heard of Mickey's accident. I didn't know him personally at the time, but remember thinking of his influence on our industry. In case you've been on a different planet I will fill you in on that history.

It was Mickey's famous club, Gilley's, that became so popular everyone wanted to visit at least once in their lifetime. The idea for the movie "Urban Cowboy" was born in the club outside Houston (Pasadena, Texas actually) and eventually the movie starring Debra Winger and John Travolta became a cult classic. His music and style was easily identifiable. Some musical genius named it "countrypolitan" (whatever that is?). I call it hard-drivin' classic country rock. It is honky-tonk music with a swagger. Love it. His first hit among many was *Room Full of Roses* back in the early 70's.

He came by his musical heritage honestly. His famous cousins, Jerry Lee Lewis, and Jimmy Swaggart, also grew up singin' and playin' in Assembly of God churches in their hometown communities in Louisiana. Mickey was born in Natchez, Mississippi but raised in Ferriday, Louisiana. Each of the famous cousins grew up playing the piano "by ear" in church. If you could play and sing at least 30 minutes during the 'altar call' for every service, you were considered a great church musician. Mickey's mother who was a "Lewis" was also musical and encouraged him to always "follow the Lord, and follow the music," in that order.

Mickey admired country artists Ernest Tubb, Hank Thompson, Hank Williams, and Webb Pierce, but they took a back seat to his admiration for his own cousin, Jerry Lee Lewis. Mickey was doing construction work (for $1.25 an hour) in Houston, while Jerry Lee was becoming an international rock n' roll star in the '50's. On one visit, the young Mickey accompanied Jerry Lee to the airport. He says that Jerry Lee pulled out a wad of bills. (Mickey says it *looked* like a wad of $100 bills – it could have just been a $100 bill on top). Anyway, Mickey saw Jerry Lee peal off that $100 bill while at the airport and that was it. He determined right then he would make it or break it in the music business.

That road would not be easy. In fact, Mickey played seamy joints and greasy dives all over the country sometimes playing for just gas money to get to the next place.

Mickey states he should have probably been more present in his children's lives (three sons and a daughter) when they were younger, but he felt he was providing for his family by being "on the road." His oldest son, Michael was born when Mickey was only seventeen years old. They basically grew up together.

He was a hard working entertainer whose love of music was contagious. He connected with the hard-working, hard- living crowd who appreciated the transparency of his songs and the pure vocal renditions. His reputation, persistence, and talent led him finally to the success he sought.

After partnering to open up Gilley's (known as the "world's biggest honky-tonk) in 1971, he would have a string of hits following *Room Full of Roses*. 1976 was a banner year for Mickey. He was named Entertainer of the Year among many other honors. The hits kept coming. One of my favorites is his rendition of the soul tune, *Stand by Me*. No one sings it like Mickey.

Through the 80's as country music leaned toward more of a "pop" sound, Mickey adjusted and remained connected with his audience and produced marketable, popular music. Then, Gilley's, the iconic home of the original 'mechanical bull' craze, caught fire and was mostly destroyed. Mickey explored new avenues for musical relevance as the country music scene continued to evolve.

Branson, Missouri was beginning to draw big names to the little resort town nestled in the foothills of the Ozarks. The strip on Highway 76 boasted new theatres owned by people with famous names like Andy Williams, Bobby Vinton, The Osmonds, Jim Stafford, and Dolly Parton bought a theatre there to house her 'Dixie Stampede' show. Great blue grass artists, family acts, gospel groups, others including the Lawrence Welk family also established their own theatres and called Branson 'home.' Among the first to explore the Branson venue for a permanent theatre was Mickey Gilley.

Gilley's Theatre in Branson opened and drew large crowds from the beginning. They came to hear the country crooner sing his hits and tickle the ivories as only he could. To this day, Gilley's is one of the most popular shows on the Branson strip. Mickey also loved to golf and when he wasn't rehearsing or performing, he would be on the golf course. He said his goal was for his score to match his age (74) and he was hitting that mark quite often before the accident. He misses the game a great deal.

This is where I come in. (You knew it had to be coming, right?). When Mickey was injured he realized that to keep the doors of his theatre open he was going to have to have others cover for him for a while. His calls to friends in the business were met by country stars eager to fill the schedule for a few months until Mickey could return.

I'm sorry to say I had not known or even met Mickey until just before we were scheduled to play his theatre. We had similar philosophies about entertaining. His professionalism went far beyond just showing up to perform; he always gives an audience what they came for: a great show, a good time, all out effort, and most of all, he genuinely cares about connecting with them. Mickey had some very nice things to say about me after he saw our show at a neighboring theatre and we were booked to perform at Gilley's. I appreciate any compliment from Mickey Gilley and take it to heart. The man knows what he's talking about – he has worked with the best in the industry. We hit it off from the start and it is my privilege to call him a friend.

As I got to know Mickey, I began to observe first hand how he handled this latest "mountain" in his life. Truth is, I never detected one ounce of self-pity, complaining, or defeatist attitude. This isn't the first physical mountain he has had to climb. He jokes, that he is "working on his eighth life."

He had heart surgery back in the 60's. There had also been a routine facial surgery that went terribly wrong. A surgeon severed the wrong artery and he actually "flatlined" on the operating table. Whew, another close call.

Then, a year before his back injury, Mickey had a shunt inserted to relieve hydrocephalus (fluid) on his brain. For some time, Mickey had been afflicted by a troublesome dizziness and weakness that caused him to physically shake and even lose his balance at times. He recalled the hurtful accusation when some theatre goers reported he was drunk while performing, when actually the stumbles and loss of memory were due to this condition. He had also experienced two airplane crashes, which now he attributes to poor perception and the imbalance caused by the hydrocephalus. When he sought medical help, the problem was discovered and the shunt was inserted. Mickey talks about the immediate euphoria of feeling 100% better. "All of a sudden, I felt like Superman," he said.

But, this newest mountain, the spinal injury, has been the toughest "row to hoe" for the star who just doesn't know how to quit. He never even considers retirement. He says, "If I ever retire, you might as well put me in a box right then." So, true to form, he continues to do what he has done since he was eleven years old. He entertains because it is in his blood – he simply *must* do it.

Mickey keeps a busy schedule of treatments each week from his home in Houston, including strength training, reflexology and acupuncture. He is able now to walk 150 feet or so, before having to rest. He is grateful that he can drive also, but can't drive too far for too long. The overwhelming physical challenge is that his strength is so limited. The doctors remain positive and so does Mickey.

Vivian, Mickey's wife of forty-two years, heads up a loving family support system. He refers to his oldest son, Michael as his "angel." Michael has been there throughout this difficult time and continues to take on the work of keeping his dad's affairs in order. His other children are equally supportive and caring.

Hope you make it to Branson to see Mickey's show. You will see the man come to the stage, wearing that little boy grin we know so well. It takes a moment to get used to seeing him somewhere other than behind the piano, but for now another takes that role. The voice hasn't changed, nor has his heart for the music. After a song or two, he fills the audience in on the injury, then jokes at the end of the explanation, "So folks, if you need something moved, call 'Two Men and a Truck' – please don't call me!" The audience laughs and immediately receives and appreciates the efforts of this country music veteran – always the ultimate entertainer. He then informs them of what the doctor is saying about his recovery to which he quips, "Shoot, pretty soon, I'll be running around here like Neal McCoy, high-fiving all of you out there!" It wouldn't surprise me a bit.

Mickey Gilley's spiritual center is apparent. He does not take one day for granted. He clearly believes that God has spared him many times for purposes he one day hopes to fully understand. I don't pretend to know why Mickey must climb this mountain, but climb he does. And it is the passion and pure love of the music that pushes him upward one step at a time.

At the close of each show, when Mickey says thanks to his audience he always adds this comment, "Folks, live like today is your last day; someday you're gonna be right!"

"You know what?" he said recently, "that's what I want on my gravestone someday – *He lived each day, like it was his last and finally it really was.*'"

To keep going in the face of any adversity is the true measure of a man's integrity. With that said, Mickey Gilley is full of that kind of integrity. If someone were to ask me what quality I admire most in other artists, it would be the pride and joy they take in their work. The world needs a Mickey Gilley simply because he is the epitome of someone who wants to give his best and sees his ability to still perform as a genuine blessing.

Happiness is an internal gift. No one can give it to us, no physical possession can substitute for it. I have never seen a man as happy as Mickey Gilley doing what he loves to do. He gets it. He knows the simple satisfaction that comes through a lifetime of making music and pleasing an audience. He loves his work. And something tells me he will be doing it long after most of us hang it up. Again, I hope so, buddy, I really hope so.

I still don't understand why Mickey has to climb this mountain at this point in his life, but maybe part of it is because others need to see him try. I know I gain the courage to overcome my day to day battles when I observe Mickey facing the battle of a lifetime with so much courage and hope.

The chorus of the song that inspired this book makes me think of Mickey. The words are:

> *Give me a new mountain to climb*
> *Tell me you don't think I can do it*
> *And I'll fool you every time.*
> *Give me a challenge I accept it*
> *Body, heart, and mind*
> *A New Mountain to Climb*

Thanks for being an inspiration to so many, Mickey. By the way, I promise I won't be calling you to help me move furniture anytime soon.

~ Neal

"Our American story, for generations, is of a people who seek to move forward. A people who look at a mountain and worry not about the tough climb ahead, but dream about the view from the summit."

—Bill Owens

"The man who removes a mountain begins by carrying away small stones."

—William Faulkner

YOU DON'T CHOOSE
THE MOUNTAIN,
IT CHOOSES YOU

Alan Babin, Jr.

> *"Great things are done when men and mountains meet."*
> —*William Blake*

I am unashamedly patriotic – I choke up when I hear the scratchy recording of the 'Star Spangled Banner' at Little League games. Like you, I wept and prayed after September 11, 2001, and then I wanted to do something during the days that followed. So, when given the opportunity to be involved in the USO tours my friend, Wayne Newton was putting together – I didn't hesitate. Entertaining our troops has been a great privilege and the stories from our experiences would make a book in itself. I gained a new perspective on the special fiber of our young people who lay their lives on the line every day. In all my tours overseas, in hundreds of discussions with soldiers, I have never heard one complaint, one doubt, one hesitation about their service and commitment to the war or our country.

Recently, I was invited to perform at the Annual Hand in Hand Purple Heart event in Branson, Missouri which honors all Purple Heart recipients. General Douglas MacArthur was instrumental in reestablishing the award to commemorate George Washington's birthday back in 1932 (that is why Washington's profile is on the medal). It is awarded to any soldier whose "wounds or death were sustained in action against an enemy of the United States." One such honoree is Alan Babin, Jr.

Alan's story is one of miraculous survival. I was privileged to meet Alan and his parents at the Purple Heart event mentioned above and knew that his story had to be included. His wounds in Iraq earned him the right to our nation's Purple Heart, but if God awards medals, (and I believe He does), Alan's parents and sister will also receive awards that will be specially designed to symbolize a love so intense, it refused to give up on their only son and brother.

~ Neal

"When preparing to climb a mountain, pack a light heart."

—Dan May

It was close to dawn on March 31, 2003 when a young private by the name of Alan Babin, lifted slightly from the drainage ditch, to view his surroundings. Back home in Texas, before deployment, he had been on a strenuous exercise regime to be in shape should he need to carry a wounded soldier or hike for miles into the desert, or outrun enemy gunfire. He must have felt prepared as he clutched the bag of medical supplies he carried. As the 82nd Airborne's only medic, his eyes took in the bridge across the river running close by the town of Samawah, Iraq. He saw minarets spiking upward above flat roofed buildings, as he peaked out from the tall grass. Then the gunfire broke out with a vengeance. The barrage of bullets, mortars and grenades seemed to come from the buildings in the distance. Then Pfc. Alan Babin heard the call for a medic. Rising from his position he saw Pfc. Joe Heit go down and Babin's instincts kicked into gear. He began to run to where Heit had fallen, about 15 feet away, when suddenly he was knocked to the ground himself. A blast left a huge gaping hole to his mid section – the injuries sustained were massive: 90% of his stomach was obliterated; the spleen, liver, intestines and pancreas were also involved. Alan would not know until later that Heit, the soldier he was running to help, had only sustained minor injuries. It wouldn't have mattered; Alan was doing what his training had taught him to do.

Mercifully, a helicopter arrived and another medic ran to check Alan's vital signs. They were not good. Alan was unresponsive, no diastolic pulse, close to losing consciousness; blood poured from under the bandages other soldiers had hastily applied to the hole in the middle where his stomach used to be. The medic thought it was imperative to try and keep Alan awake so the morphine he carried was never administered. He kept yelling at Alan to stay awake, even slapping him gently, fearful that Alan might never awaken if allowed to sleep. Alan was loaded aboard the helicopter and flown to the nearest hospital and air base.

At home, miles away on the other side of the world, his mother, Rosalinda Babin (Rosie), cheerfully answered her kitchen phone in Round Rock, Texas. Then, realizing that the call was from Alan's unit commander she began to make notes with a shaking hand: "Alan wounded…gunshots to abdomen…medevaced to field hospital…currently stable…will have Alan call when able…" The shock set in, but the report of "stable" was reassuring. After informing friends and family, she kept the lines free, but days passed with no further word.

Rosie says that these first days were some of the hardest. There were dark, weary days when she prayed for any word on her son's condition. Finally, after 10 days the family learned Alan was on a medical ship in the Gulf, the USNS Comfort, undergoing rounds of surgeries. Every night around the same time (midnight) surgeons would call and give the details of the horrific surgeries, kidney failure, dialysis, ventilator support, low platelet counts, health continuing to decline. Added to that, his heart rate was not stabilized, there was severe injury to pancreas and bowel, infection was a threat, and he remained heavily sedated. The early report of Alan's condition being "stable" was erroneous, his condition status from the beginning was "critical."

While on the hospital ship surgeons performed almost daily surgery trying to piece together Alan's mangled intestines. While being fed from a tube, liquid would seep from yet undetected holes in his intestines. Bacteria caused high fever, blood count was dangerously low, and his heart rate was more than 140 beats per minute. Doctors held little hope that he would make it.

The usual robust and lively Babin household became eerily quiet as Rosie, husband Alan Sr, and their daughter, (Alan's younger sister, Christy, 16), awaited further word. Morgue-like the family barely functioned and the frustration of little information made the hours excruciating.

Christy wrote tenderly and hopefully to her big brother,

"Hey Big Bro! Well, you've pulled off your biggest stunt, and I wasn't there to try it too! Of course, this is a lot bigger than riding our bikes up the slanted tree on Pickwick or putting a battery on our tongue to see who could hold out the longest! Nope, what you've done, what you've been through was much greater than any dare someone could pull out of their imagination, even a triple dog dare. You chose to survive, and I've never been so proud of anybody or any cause as I am now."

Christy's letter was read at Alan's bedside by a friend of the family, a nurse who happened to be stationed on the ship. The friend was so moved by the words, her eyes filled with tears and she passed the letter to another nurse who continued to read:

"…you let me tag along for my first fishing trip. You showed me all the forts you all had built, even let me in on some of your secrets…but the thing I remember most was getting lost while we were back there…you cried. You cried because I was lost, even though it was just for a little while. When I found out what had happened to you, I cried too. I cried because you were lost, even though it was just for a little while. Alan, you are the most important person in my life. You have never asked me to do anything that I'm not capable of, nor I of you. So, I'm going to keep things simple and just ask you to come home. I need to see your face soon, so stay strong and feel the desire to live. I know you'll get through this and come out stronger because you're my big brother. I love you very much and hope you can feel that, even across the world. Love, your lil' sis, Christy.

"P.S. I'm 16 now, so you better be ready for a lot of ride-alongs when you get home!"

Rosie recalls a morning in April during those traumatic days. She was driving into the office of the accounting firm where she worked in Austin, (the work was a much needed diversion from staring at the phone all day). She was praying while driving as was her usual custom, when she was overcome with tears and the unbelievable pain of fear and possible loss. She cried to God, "If you want Alan this much, please, just take him, but stop the pain he is going through."

The next day, a surgeon reported that Alan had "turned the corner" and now they would be doing everything they could to send him home. Somehow, Alan had held on.

Alan could not speak but when his mom would call, nurses held the phone to his ear, while his mother spoke to him and he would recognize her voice and clearly understood what she was saying.

After two weeks on the ship he was flown to Germany for more treatment, and then later transferred to Walter Reed Army Medical Center in Washington. Out of thousands of US military casualties from Iraq, Alan would hold a record for the longest hospital stay. He endured seventy surgeries over a period of seven months.

Rosie resigned her job and moved to Washington. She became a permanent fixture at the Walter Reed Army Medical Center in Washington, hardly ever leaving Alan's side. She sat up her computer in Alan's room and kept a detailed diary and corresponded with family and friends via email. She pored through web sites and learned the medical terminology for all that Alan was battling. She kept a fierce eye on her son and held doctors and nurses accountable for his care. She learned to care for Alan's tracheotomy, changed the dressings on his wound, massaged his limbs and kept bedsores at bay. She also became a counselor and friend to many other soldiers and their families. Some of those brave young soldiers did not make it. Month after month Alan had to stay while others came and went. When depression and/or fatigue would plague Rosie, it was Christy, who reminded her mother they were blessed that Alan had survived; many families were not so lucky.

After seven long months at Alan's bedside, Rosie received word she was hoping against hope she'd never hear. She was devastated to hear Alan had indeed suffered, "traumatic brain injury." Up to that point she had seen young men returning from Iraq with "traumatic brain injuries." There were soldiers whose craniums were blown completely away, blinded warriors with little or no family to help them through. She had even held the hand of a sergeant who had died from his brain injury; she was the only one present when the young man passed away. One positive note is that doctors have reported more soldiers are surviving serious, massive injuries sustained in the current Mideast conflicts, unlike the wars of the past.

Rosie remained convinced and felt in time Alan would be able to communicate. He could already be observed attempting to form words; he just didn't have the strength to push the words out. Then, after he was finally transferred to the Rehab center in Texas, his raspy, rough voice could be heard trying to express himself. Working with a therapist he learned to listen to the therapist ask questions and then the therapist would give possible answers and each answer was assigned a number. Holding up his fingers, Alan began to pick the correct answer to the questions, 1, 2 or 3.

During one of those sessions Alan indicated he had full memory of his childhood and all the way through basic training, but he did not remember Iraq. He didn't remember even deploying to Kuwait. It is probably for the best.

The family rejoiced when Alan was finally cleared to be cared for in the home, but the family knew it would be an intense level of care and support for the young man who was everyone's hero.

So what is life like now for the Babin family, 7 years after Alan was wounded?

Younger sis, Christy, loves running and plans to participate in the Marine Corps Marathon in Washington later this year. She wants to obtain an RN degree and then pursue a registered dietician degree. A fan of Texas A & M, Christy aspires to get an "Aggie" ring as soon as possible. She lives at home and often travels with her mom and Alan to Wounded Warrior events. They have many "girl talks" about Christy's future. Rosie feels somewhat regretful for the time she was away from Christy during her High School years, caring for Alan. But Christy is adamant, "I couldn't even marry anyone who doesn't understand Alan's needs and would not be able or willing to assist in his recovery." Such words bring solace to the Texas mom's heart. "Those are the grateful, sad, happy, my-cup-runneth-over, joyful days when I cry myself to sleep in disbelief that I have had a part in raising children that put others' needs before their own."

Alan lives comfortably at home with the assistance of a home health aide. Rosie has the routine down pat: She has a cup of tea while Alan wakes. After quiet time for prayer and devotions, she goes through multiple procedures necessary to caring for Alan including; bladder/bowel management, getting him showered, shaved, and dressed. A ceiling lift transfers Alan from bed to wheelchair. Then the bed is made while Alan brushes his teeth, then Rosie showers while Alan has his coffee and light breakfast. The home health care program includes occupational, physical and speech therapy, and upper-body strengthening for wheelchair accessible weight training.

Rosie is chauffeur for Alan, making sure he gets to VA appointments, haircuts, shopping, meeting up with friends. The wheelchair accessible van has been a blessing. (One interesting note: Texas icon and former presidential candidate, Ross Perot donated the first van to the family upon hearing of Alan's injuries). Rosie also works with Alan on the Wii, plays scrabble with him, and helps him with handwriting too.

Dinner for the Babins is usually a time together as a family. They have discovered that evenings are most successful when they are uncomplicated and relaxed, allowing Alan to get to bed early. While Alan falls to sleep, Rosie and Alan, Sr. carve out a few moments to share a glass of wine, and catch up with each other personally. Only then, does Rosie have opportunity to answer emails, return phone calls, journal, and watch a little television.

Rosie finds deep satisfaction accompanying Alan to meetings, (he's a member of the Texas Governor's Committee on People with Disabilities), and Wounded Warrior events, or Purple Heart programs like the one in Branson. She shares Alan's story with veterans, civic, nonprofit, and educational organizations. When Rosie and Alan appear in schools, Alan typically ends the presentation with the personal admonishment to students, "Never, never, never give up!"

A cause dear to the Babin family is the Caring Bridge web site. It is a site available to military families which became a great source of encouragement and information to Rosie and a link has been added for Alan whereby gifts or donations can be made to the organization in Alan's honor (www.caringbridge.org/tx/alansangels). Rosie added, "We also appreciate and want to be part of Neal's organization, East Texas Angel Network, because we know first hand the challenges and expenses associated with a loved one's hospitalization."

Rosie smiles when I ask how the family came to be "fans" of our music. After moving back to Texas from California in '94 one of the first concerts Rosie attended with Christy was a concert I did in Austin with LeAnn Rimes. She said she knew it would be a high-energy, fun-filled evening and it was. She and Christy stood and cheered and rocked to the music and had a great time. "We were not surprised when you were named 'Entertainer of the Year,'" she added.

Then, she spoke of our meeting in Branson. "Can you imagine how beyond-thrilled I was to see you sitting at the front of the theater in Branson at the Purple Heart program? I could hardly wait to introduce you to Alan. I was so thankful you were there to honor our Nation's heroes and, true to your reputation and USO spirit, you were there to support the guys."

I wondered if Rosie had ever been angry at God for Alan's injuries. Did she ever have a moment when the mountain that chose them, seemed so huge and unfair, she wanted to simply give up? Her answer is unedited:

"No, Neal – I have never been mad at God for what happened to Alan. Before he was wounded, friends and family can probably tell you stories of my praising God for a "boring life" whenever we heard others reporting bad news. If anything, I considered our journey with Alan a test of our "easy/boring" lives we once knew. I was blessed to have found a personal relationship with Christ at the age of 23 and have spent the greater part of my adult life praising Him. How could I suddenly blame Him for a decision our son made to protect and defend our Constitution?

As veterans, Al and I wonder if we over-glamorized our service during peace-time; however, Alan made the decision to serve knowingly and willingly after the events of September 11, 2001 and we supported him in the decision. Granted, I wanted to wring his chicken-neck and hug him at the same time!

So as for giving up? That has *never* been an option for me. If I give up – Alan will give up. God preserved Alan's life for a reason and I feel led to honor it. There are days when I am beyond "dog tired" but I continue to be inspired by my son's courage to claw his way back to health. Seven years after he was wounded, he continues to strive for more recovery, to smile at the people in his life and to inspire me to advocate strongly for him and his fellow veterans, every day."

At the Purple Heart concert, Rosie tells me everyone in the whole family are fans, including Alan. I lean down and reach for the hand of the frail young man sitting in the wheel chair. With halting speech, but great smile he greets me. In turn, I am speechless for a moment. I wish I had adequate words to express my thanks to Alan. How do you thank someone for being there at that place at that time and consequently, taking the bullet for you; for us?

Sometimes in life, we don't get to choose the mountain; it chooses us. The Babins faced life's biggest mountain and when the mountain seemed insurmountable, prayers and hopes moved heaven and with time and patience, the impossible became possible.

I was the most impatient kid ever and waiting for anything was hard for me. As an adult I still have to remind myself that patience is a virtue. More I think about it, the waiting had to be the hardest part for Alan's family. The waiting for word of his condition, then having to wait to see if he had even survived the surgeries must have required the greatest degree of patience. The waiting had to be a thousand times harder than anything requiring action.

Alan is a real American hero and has the Purple Heart to prove it. But aren't there several heroes here? There is a determined mom, a devoted dad, and a proud sister who stood and waited, didn't lose heart and never lost hope, and they continue to live each day to cheer on Alan's victories, however small. These are grand acts of heroism. This family stood together, and when the mountain chose them, they were not afraid of the climb.

~ Neal

"The restless craving in the souls of men spurs them to climb and to seek the mountain view."

—Ella Wheeler Wilcox

"Winners take time to relish their work, knowing that scaling the mountain is what makes the view from the top so exhilarating."

—Denis Waitley

STORM ON THE MOUNTAIN

Sandy Henry

"The storms of life prove the strength of our anchor."
—Unknown

There are some mysteries in life and nature I will never be able to wrap my mind around. As dangerous as they can be, tornadoes have always held a fascination for me. Sometimes the east Texas wind can kick up a fuss and spin some devastating twisters in this area of the country. The most unusual time however, is just before the storm. An eerie calm signals change coming as warm breezes turn cooler and the sky blackens toward the west. Then the clouds start churning, the wind picks up, and folks head toward a safe place because the storm is heading our way.

The May 3rd, 1999 tornado that targeted Oklahoma has been recorded as the most devastating on record. It was more than a mile wide and cut a swath through the state that left forty-eight dead and hundreds injured. Entire neighborhoods and thousands of homes were destroyed. Among the lives taken by the storm was a young man in his prime, David Henry. David and his wife, Sandy had planned a night out, but the approaching storm changed their plans and their lives forever.

When I first spoke to Sandy, the pain was still apparent in her soft-spoken, Oklahoma drawl. Fresh tears fell as she recounted the events on the day of May 3rd. When you love someone deeply, the void is never filled when they are gone – you just simply somehow go on living without them. Any of us would be blessed to know a love as deep and rich as the one shared between David and Sandy Henry. The tornado did not erase countless memories, or diminish the joy they knew every day.

There is a line in the song for which this book is titled, "A New Mountain to Climb." It says, "When storm clouds hang on the horizon and a bitter wind intends to blow...." Below is Sandy's story about that bitter wind that blew across Oklahoma and claimed the life of her husband – her best friend.

~ Neal

"There are two kinds of climbers; those whose hearts sing when they're in the mountains, and all the rest."

—Alex Lowe

By late Monday afternoon on May 3, 1999 the beautiful warm weather that had graced Oklahoma for the past few days, turned eerily cooler. The sky became an ominous mix of yellows and grays. People making the drive home from work, kept a wary eye on the churning clouds to the south as they listened to radio reports of a storm approaching from the southwest. Weather predictors were saying the storm was growing larger and could be in the process of forming tornadoes. The track of the storm was headed in a diagonal direction toward south Oklahoma City.

David and Sandy Henry were fans of the Oklahoma City Blazers hockey team and had plans to attend the league's playoff game that evening. Sandy offered to prepare something light for dinner before they left home for the game downtown. The couple settled on peanut butter and jelly sandwiches to hold them until they got to the game. Around 6 p.m. as they finished off the sandwiches, their attention was turned to the television reports of the oncoming storm.

If you live in "tornado alley" long enough you become conditioned to the many storm watches, alerts, tornado watches and warnings. But, this time it sounded serious. David made a quick call to his mother and father, and a brother, Mark, living in the area, making sure they had heard about the on-coming storm. All assured him they would take necessary storm precautions.

For sixteen years David had worked for Oklahoma Gas and Electric Company. He was currently the material coordinator of procurement for the company. Besides working full time, he was finishing up a degree from the University of Central Oklahoma with plans to graduate the next spring with a degree in purchasing. The former high school valedictorian was a model student and was breezing through college courses with perfect grades. He enjoyed fishing, also football and golf, but he especially loved hockey and was looking forward to the game downtown at the Myriad that evening.

Sandy and David stepped onto their back patio and saw what looked to be a huge "black rain cloud" on the ground, filling up the horizon to the southwest. They didn't realize they were actually staring at a tornado whose force and speed would violently make their doorstep in just seconds.

The decision was immediately made that the couple would not venture out. Instead, they would hunker down with their dachshund, Sammy, (a wedding gift to Sandy from David), and wait out the storm. David quickly gathered blankets and pillows and they headed toward what they thought to be the safest room; a bathroom situated in the center on the ground floor of their two-story home.

Pulling the blankets and pillows over their heads, the couple crouched together, with David hovering over Sandy in the bathtub. David was cradling the dog with one arm and Sandy with the other. There was a brief moment of playful nudging and even a quick kiss and an "I love you" before the violent impact.

There was a ferocious shaking, and then the house literally imploded. Everything went black. The tub was moving. There were deafening, screeching sounds as the home was ripped from its foundation and crumbled all around them. Asked to comment later on what the tornado sounded like, Sandy would say, "You know, the loud mega blow-dryers at the car wash? That is what it sounded like, only magnified hundreds of times."

The couple and their dog were lifted up and thrown from the tub and sent flying through the debris. Huge shards of glass and plaster and brick swirled around, mixed with a choking, thick dust. Sandy heard the dog moan from somewhere nearby, and then heard a raspy, weak voice,

"I love you, Sandy. It's not supposed to be like this ... I love you."

She was frantic. From where she had fallen, she couldn't see her husband, but heard his words and turned toward them. Barely able to see through the debris, she could make out David's forearm extending out from fallen sheet rock and mounds and mounds of debris. She could not reach him, her legs wouldn't move. She began to scream hysterically,

"Help us ... someone please! Help us! We are hurt! David! David! God, help us! Please help us!"

Then, Sandy lay still. She never lost consciousness, but shock was setting in. A million particles rained down from the sky as another fear overtook her. The strong odor of a ruptured gas line jolted her back to reality as she began to scream out again. Within ten minutes, but what seemed like an eternity, Sandy heard the sounds of people running, shouting, neighbors calling out, someone reaching to dig her out, sirens. Just as she was being lifted on to a stretcher she saw workers removing large pieces of wood and sheetrock that had fallen on David and then she glimpsed his face for a brief moment. Her mind said, "He's gone," but her heart would not accept it. "They will be loading him up, too. I will see him again in just a few minutes," she said to herself.

They took her first to a triage unit set up at the nearby high school. Then after being checked out for injuries, a kind couple drove her to the closest hospital (Southwest Medical Center) where she thought David would be arriving anytime. She kept asking, "Is my husband here? Please where is my husband."

The answer was always guarded, "We are not sure where he will be taken. There are three hospitals receiving tornado victims tonight. We will try to let you know."

Unable to reach the couple by phone, Sandy's mother had also made her way to the hospital and was there awaiting word when Sandy arrived. Once at the hospital, Sandy realized she didn't have any identification, no purse, no credit cards, nothing but the clothes on her back. She had miraculously escaped injury with only a slight cut and abrasion to one arm.

David's mother and father arrived at the hospital a few moments later. Mr. and Mrs. Henry kept asking Sandy, "Did you see David? Did he look hurt?"

"Yes," Sandy answered, not wanting to share a growing premonition, "David is hurt. He is hurt really bad."

The wait at the hospital was excruciating. Then, around 3 a.m. Sandy decided to go to the Henry's home to clean up, take a shower. Sleep was out of the question. David's mother, who was already struggling with the onset of dementia, was inconsolable, yet Sandy wanted to be at their home in case someone sent word of David's status. David's father would pass away barely nine months later from what many would say was a broken heart.

By late that evening, a command post was set up at Oakcrest Church so that relatives could check on missing family members and make contact with them. Sandy and her in-laws made their way to the church seeking any further word about David.

People mulled about the sanctuary and grounds of the church, shock on their tear-stained faces, all desperate for word about loved ones. Children played in the hallways, while church volunteers offered hot coffee and snacks to the anxious crowd. Then around 9 the next morning, May 4th, the pastor of the church found Sandy and her family and told them they had received word about David. Guiding them into a small room, he gently delivered the news. David had been found and the medical examiner had determined he had died of asphyxiation on the scene. Most likely he had taken the brunt of the impact while attempting to protect Sandy. Sammy, the couple's beloved pet was also found dead nearby. David's fragile mother screamed in denial and begged that it not be so, "No, no!"

"I love you Sandy... It's not supposed to be like this." The words kept playing, tearing Sandy's heart out again and again as she gasped for air. Her body shook and her

thoughts were chaotic: *Where is he now? Where did they take him? What do I do? David, I can't do this? I cannot make it without you. I need to get some clothes from home – wait, our home is gone. I have nothing. A funeral? I have to plan David's funeral. Oh, God – why? I'm so scared.*

Then, a heavy darkness like she had never known, blacker than the tornado itself, enfolded Sandy as she sank to her knees and cried until it seemed humanly impossible to shed one more tear.

The next few days were a blur. Sandy cannot recall certain details during those first few days following David's death. She stayed with his parents during that time. The mind has a way of numbing itself when dealing with loss and Sandy says she was in a dense fog most of the time. A couple of articles would appear in local papers focusing on The Henrys but Sandy would not even recall speaking with reporters afterwards.

Somehow, the closed casket memorial service was planned, but she wouldn't recall making the plans. The service would be held at the funeral home chapel instead of the church where David and Sandy attended and were married. Sandy couldn't bear the thought of having memories of their wedding and David's funeral at the same church.

She remembered there was a pale pink dress suit that had been sent to the dry cleaners. It was retrieved so she could wear it to the funeral. A nephew shopped for shoes, a friend came over to do her hair and make-up. And on a beautiful sunny day, with the chapel packed with family, friends, co-workers, professors, David

Henry, a bright, promising, loving man was remembered and honored.

Sandy sat between her mother and David's grandmother and tried to maintain emotional control during the service. At 36 years of age, she had lost her sweetheart, her husband, her best friend. She thought about meeting David on the first day she worked for Rudy's Bestyet Grocery Store. He asked her out that day. They would be engaged for three years as Sandy finished college. The memories, like a movie, begin to play in her mind as the service continued: Flowers he sent for no reason, romantic cards, the surprises Sandy treasured, a new fishing pole; the meals he would prepare just for her; deep sea fishing trips they loved, camping trips to Lake Tenkiller; trying out new restaurants, places they wanted to visit. Tears spotted her pink suit as they fell silently.

Words were spoken, prayers were offered, music was played ...

In the arms of the angel, may you find some comfort here.

Eventually the gravestone for David would include a photo of the smiling couple, birth and death dates, and this inscription:

"Believe and have faith in all you do,
and angels will guide a path for you."

At first, Sandy visited David's grave site two or three times a day. The shock was wearing off but a profound loneliness set in. She hadn't lived alone for over fifteen years. She moved into a small apartment and purchased replacement furniture. Oklahoma City Public Schools, where Sandy worked in the Finance department, granted her almost three months leave. She went for long drives, tried to reconnect with friends, saw a grief counselor, and even tried a support group for a while.

One of the most difficult days for Sandy came about two weeks after the tornado, when she had to meet officials of FEMA at the site where her home had stood. Entering the neighborhood was like looking over the bombed out villages of World War II. Trees were stripped and toppled. The streets were unrecognizable. Where lovely homes once stood, the lots were full of what looked like tons of twisted metal, broken bricks, sheetrock.

Then she saw what was left of her home at 1012 S.W. 126th. The sight was horrendous. It reminded her of giant shards of toothpicks piled on one another. A neighbor's pick up had been thrown like a toy car into the middle of what once was her living room. The stench from the accumulating debris was strong as demolition crews began their work. With papers signed, Sandy turned, walked away and never looked back again.

A few items would be salvaged by family and friends who spent hours searching for lost mementos. A set of Mickey Mouse characters their niece and nephew brought back from Disneyland were found and David's prized CD collection survived intact. Most precious was their wedding photo album, buried under mounds of debris, yet it looked as if it hadn't been touched.

Forty eight people lost their lives in the May 3rd tornado, and hundreds more were injured. The F5 monster measured more than a mile wide and reached the highest speed (310 mph) ever recorded for a tornado. Thousands of homes were lost or damaged. The state reeled with the devastation but realized it could have been so much worse without the early warning systems in place.

Now several years later, Sandy Henry lives in a new home about three miles from the home that was destroyed. Don (David's cousin) and Darlene Chesser, builders in the area, had Sandy's new home built at no cost to her. She is very grateful for such a generous gift.

She never considered moving out of the area – she has roots here. There is a "safe room" in her new house and when the sky darkens and tornado sirens blare, she takes shelter there. She refuses to live in fear however, of the storms that routinely make their way across the Oklahoma landscape every spring.

Other friends, co-workers, along with the Oklahoma Red Cross made donations to Sandy and she remains thankful for the tremendous outpouring of love and support she received during that time. After the insurance proceeds came in, she established an ongoing scholarship fund at the University of Central Oklahoma in David's name.

There were some tough decisions Sandy made to cope with losing David. "I had to find a new 'normal'" she said. "I had to find out who I was without him. I had to establish a new identity. And then there was the guilt. A beautiful man died saving me. Why was I left here? What is the purpose of my life?

"Of course, I was angry and I battled with my faith for a time, questioning God's love for me and how He could allow this to happen. I began to realize that my life was spared for purposes beyond my understanding. I determined to make a choice to survive every day.

"I made a choice to return to work. For several months I poured myself into my job as never before just to fill up the time. I am grateful for my job and the people I work with who understood I would have some really bad days.

"I also made a choice to face well-meaning friends and family who wanted to feel sorry for me and, or take care of me. I had to explain that there were some things I didn't need to hear early on, like, 'Sandy, there will be someone else for you someday.' Or, 'You need to get on with your life, get over this – David would want that.'

"I chose to end some relationships. Other couples David and I saw as a couple, were still couples. I was the odd one out. Trying to act as if the make up of the group was still the same was not working. It made me and them feel uncomfortable. Everyone was trying too hard to ignore the elephant in the room. I made new friends and drew my family in closer.

"I made a choice only recently to see other people. I do get lonely, and I have opened myself up to the pos-sibility that I could date and enjoy another man's company. Ultimately I know David would want me happy above all else," she said.

David's nieces and nephew, Scott, Angela and Shelby (whom the couple treated as their own) are now all grown up with families of their own. They still speak of and miss their "Unc" as they called David. Sandy knows he would be so proud of these great kids.

I wondered if there were any regrets with her relationship with David. Were there things left unsaid? Things she wish she had done? Were there any unresolved issues? Her answer was immediate. "No regrets. We stayed up to date with each other and expressed love and passion for each other often and sincerely."

Sandy Henry smiles widely and her eyes twinkle at the memories of a "once-in-a-lifetime" love. She would implore us to never waste one day, and to hold each moment precious because nothing else is promised us. Her hope is that others facing such crisis will know they are stronger than they ever believed themselves to be.

Tucked inside the wedding album Sandy treasures is a card David sent her with a personal note after she had been away on a trip. He wrote:

I have missed you more than I ever expected. I'm glad you're home. To feel you in my arms again makes me feel complete. I love you, today and always. Love, David

David's final act of love was to make sure Sandy found safety in those arms once again.

Not far from where David Henry lost his life a memorial marker has been installed. It says:

> *Dedicated to the resilience of all Oklahomans.*
>
> *To those who perished and those who overcame the largest outbreak of tornados in Oklahoma history on May 3, 1999.*

I say, "Amen." Sandy Henry is one of those "overcomers." She still visits David's grave on special occasions. For the rest of her life she will thank God for the unique love she and David enjoyed. (And, I love this part.) In 1994 I recorded a song that was special to me and my wife, only to find out is was also special to David and Sandy Henry. The title of the song is "Heaven." Sandy says the song was a perfect expression of their commitment to each other. The chorus of the song goes:

> *I thank God that there's a heaven,*
>
> *A place to go when my days are through*
>
> *I do not have to go far to get there, not yet*
>
> *Cause "Heaven" is at home with you.*

When the day is a little tough to get through, Sandy thinks of the song, looks heavenward and smiles. And somewhere

David Henry must be smiling back with that big, mischievous grin and there is not a hint of a storm on his horizon.

~ Neal

"The mountains are calling and I must go."

—John Muir

"My father considered a walk among the mountains, the equivalent of church going."

—Aldous Huxley

BUTTERFLIES ON THE MOUNTAIN

Emily Snider

> *Love is like a butterfly: It goes where it pleases and it pleases wherever it goes.*
>
> *—Unknown*

The first time I saw her she was sitting in a wheelchair close to the stage at a concert in Hallsville High School in Hallsville, Texas, a town just outside of Longview. During the show, I slipped close to the edge of the stage and sang 'My Girl' to her. She was elated and afterward we took several pictures. From that day on, Emily Kathaleen Snider was a lifelong fan ... I know I have one, for sure!

One of the things I would come to learn about Emily is that her mom and dad refer to her as their "little butterfly." I don't know a whole lot about butterflies. I chased 'em as a kid. That was around the same time I was capturing lightning bugs in fruit jars. Did you know that butterflies cannot fly in temperatures below 50 degrees or that some butterflies taste with their feet? Another thing I know about

*butterflies; the struggle to become a butterfly is so intense
that it takes days to recover.*

*I would learn that Emily, like other butterflies, also had
to struggle to survive. How wonderful that God blessed her
with a great family whose love for her is limitless.*

Here is Emily's story – our "butterfly."

~ Neal

"Because it's there."

—George Leigh Mallory,
on being asked why he wanted to climb Mt. Everest

Steve and Lana Snider were not overly concerned when
informed their baby would need to be delivered by
c-section. The doctor had told the young couple that
the c-section would be necessary due to the fact that
the baby was in the breech position.

Friends and family showed up at the hospital. Lana
had experienced two previous miscarriages so everyone was excited to welcome this new little one. Their
excitement turned to concern as reports came that the
baby was in trouble. Finally, fear cancelled out any hope
for celebrations when they were told the baby was born
with spina bifida (nuero-tube defect), and had severe
hydrocephalus (water on the brain). The baby actually died twice in the delivery room. Emily Kathaleen
Snider, weighing in at ten pounds, 4 ounces, was in
extremely critical condition and was sent to a hospital

in Dallas by ambulance. She could not be life-flighted due to the severity of her back – the altitude alone could have ruptured her tiny back. Steve, Emily's dad, followed the ambulance to Dallas, and upon arrival at the hospital was immediately given a room to share with the baby. The assumption was clear; no one expected Emily to make it through the night.

The family was asking God for a miracle and Lana is quick to credit the "power of God" and Emily's own "fighting spirit" for her daughter's survival during those first days. For fifty long days the newborn lay in the Children's Medical Center in Dallas struggling to live and Steve and Lana made sure she was never alone. When finally allowed to go home with their daughter, Steve and Lana knew many surgeries would be required over the next few months.

Home for the Sniders is a small acreage that sits between Longview and Hallsville, Texas (in Harrison County, right off of Highway 80). There was only one traffic light through Hallsville until 2003. The town is expanding quickly and now there are five traffic lights. Like the majority of communities its size, the school system and related sports events, are the main attractions for the townspeople. The Sniders, who have lived on the same property for nearly forty years, marvel at how quickly the housing additions have sprung up, surrounding their acreage on all sides.

Steve Snider is a heavy equipment operator for Luminant Mining Company (for over 30 years at time of this writing). He is a burly guy with long hair and beard. His friends call him 'Wolfman.' Steve is an imposing figure, until you strike up a conversation and his true temperament is revealed. This gentle, bear of a man has a huge heart and lives for his wife and daughter. He enjoys hunting and fishing, following the Dallas Cowboys, and working in his shop. Neighbors love Steve and know him as the plain spoken man who has a nickname for everyone. He owns a great sense of humor and easy laugh.

Lana remembers when Emily was in the hospital in Dallas. For days following her surgery, Steve sat by her bedside, so his hand touched her at all times. Emily would grab hold of his fingers tightly and Steve would lay his head down on the bed and sleep in that position for hours at a time. The couple would make the decision that Lana would stay in the home as Emily's primary care-giver, but Steve is equally and lovingly invested in his daughter.

When asked, the couple has lost count of the number of surgeries their "butterfly" has required over the years. In 1991 alone, she had four operations in 22 hours. (She had lost her upper body movement and speech and had to be tube fed during this period). The list of surgeries would include several eye surgeries, brain surgeries, surgery to repair a broken leg from riding on the school bus, tissue expanders to stretch skin to remove scar tissue, jaw surgery to realign her jaw and teeth, back surgery because of pressure sores, IV treatments for bladder infections, and many other surgeries and complications.

Emily is paralyzed from the breast down and must use a wheelchair for mobility. Also four to five times a day, Lana dutifully does cath procedures, to make sure Emily's lower digestive tract is functioning properly. It is just part of the every day routine for this mother who sees her daughter as a true "gift from God." And that's not just lip service. Lana explains, "You know, all we have on earth is given to us from God to take care of while we are here, so Emily is really just on loan from God. He chose us as her parents, and we are so thankful." Emily is their only child.

From pre-school to high school, Emily attended schools in the Hallsville school system. At age 10, she and a friend attended a concert at Hallsville High School, because they heard I was performing and hadn't seen me in concert before. Another country artist from my hometown area, Ricky Lynn Gregg, performed at the same event. At some point during my set, I sang 'My Girl' to the two young ladies sitting in wheel chairs at the front of the auditorium. One of those girls was Emily Snider who became a country music fan from that day forward.

Because of Emily's love for music, the family joined our fan club base and we were delighted to see them at concerts, in Nashville at Fan Fair (CMA Music Fest), and other music events. Even before East Texas Angel Network (ETAN) was created, the Sniders were supportive and excitedly embraced Emily's love for country music.

After ETAN was created to help families with expenses related to a child's medical care, the Sniders filled out an application to be considered for assistance. Emily became one of our very first 'angels' whom we were able to help. Even when a family has some insurance it is often not nearly enough to cover the costs of caring for a child with Emily's medical needs. ETAN paid the final bill for Emily's wheelchair, and provided some money to cover travel expenses back and forth when Emily had a long hospital stay. ETAN also made payments on a van for the family to use. Later, the Snider family donated that same van back to ETAN so another family could use it.

At the age of 19 Emily would be released from hospital care following the last back surgery. Many doctors who had cared for Emily through out her life became life long friends. The family is quick to express gratefulness for The Texas Scottish Rite Hospital where Emily went often for special treatments. That same year, Emily Snider graduated from High School and her folks beamed with pride through out the ceremonies.

Emily is now a young lady, 25 years old. She spends her days at home, viewing YouTube on her laptop, watching music videos and interviews, doing "word searches" in a book, playing memory games. She enjoys watching CMT, GAC and the Food Network. Her mother makes sure that her physical therapy includes exercises to strengthen her upper body.

Lana spoke of the struggles in years past to care for Emily, "Through all the pain and suffering, God's mercy and love pulled us through. These last few years have been relatively worry free and Emily is doing fine. We do things now that we would have never done had Emily been a "normal" child. She has done many things in her life that most "normal" children never get to do. She has been the ambassadress for March of Dimes for five years and won exciting trips. Then, there are the yearly treks to Nashville for Fan Fair. Of course, there are things in her life, she will never be able to do, but we have made some wonderful memories with Emily and the years are flying by. She is a bright, alert, talkative country music fan, who loves her music and cooking shows."

The Sniders have worked hard to see that Emily's desires and wishes are fulfilled as long as it is within their power to do so. I remember watching Steve with Emily during a charity golf tournament we held a few years ago. It was hot as blazes and we had run out of golf carts for Emily to use. That wasn't a problem for Steve. There he was, pushing Emily around in her wheelchair up and down the hills, across the fairways, all the while laughing, enjoying each moment.

Steve and Lana intend to provide countless happy experiences and memorable moments for their "butterfly." Some of Emily's happiest moments grew out of her love of country music. Because of that love, we have seen Emily many times over the years. She has also met Alan Jackson, Reba, Trace Adkins, Terri Clark, Charlie Daniels, Ricky Skaggs, Sherrie Austin, Blake Shelton, Chris Young, among many others.

Before we take pictures with Emily, her mother, Lana usually instructs Emily to hold her head up for the photo by saying, "Remember, Em – skinny chin, skinny chin." Because her head is usually down a bit and over to the side, her chin can look tucked in and cramped. When her mother says this, Emily will stretch her neck up and out for the pic. So, now I remind her too, "Okay, Butterfly, 'skinny chin, skinny chin.'"

Steve and Lana Snider still have many wonderful memories to make with Emily. Their wishes for her are simple, "That she will continue to live a comfortable, joy filled life, knowing she is valued and loved beyond description." These extraordinary parents and Emily are true heroes of mine because they have discovered that when your dreams don't turn out exactly as you had hoped, you make different dreams and live life to the fullest anyway. God gave Steve and Lana a beautiful "butterfly" to nurture and enjoy and He gave Emily the courage to try out her wings every day.

Each time I am around this loving, unique family I appreciate their dedication to create memories with Emily. They are not going to miss one opportunity to enjoy life's smallest or greatest moments. What rich and satisfying times they have had and will have in the future with their special "butterfly."

Some butterflies prefer the high mountains. The lofty heights and cooler temperatures suit them just fine. Emily Snider has had to climb some pretty rough mountains in her young life but she's a "butterfly" and she takes nourishment and joy in the things the mountains have taught her. If you are ever privileged to meet Emily Kathaleen Snider, you will be blessed if she lights in your presence, even for a moment.

May the wings of the butterfly kiss the sun
And find your shoulder to light on,
To bring you luck, happiness and riches
Today, tomorrow and beyond.

Irish Blessing

~ Neal

"I am here for a purpose and that purpose is to grow into a mountain, not to shrink to a grain of sand. Henceforth, will I apply ALL my efforts to become the highest mountain of all and I will strain my potential until it cries for mercy."

—Og Mandino

"The experienced mountain climber is not intimidated by the mountain, he is inspired by it."

—William Arthur Ward

YOU BEGIN TO APPRECIATE THE MOUNTAIN

John John Youngblood

"It's not the mountain we conquer but ourselves."
—*Edmund Hillary*

I first noticed him about five years ago. It would be hard not to notice him. He had a strong upper body, but his legs were short, misshapen. He used crutches to walk. He was a friend of one of the guys in the band.

John John Youngblood started hanging around backstage, eager to help. He was from Gilmer, Texas which is about twenty miles north of Longview where I live. His love for music was obvious and he began to express his desire to work for me and the band if any opportunity arose. When my longtime merchandise guy left us, I remembered the young man with the easy smile and asked him to come along for a few gigs to see if he liked it and to see if he could handle the job.

He has become a valuable member of our team and our fans love meeting John John at the merchandise tables. John

John inspires me every day with his determination to climb mountains others said he would never be able to climb. Hope you have the great pleasure of meeting him one day.

~ Neal

Arthrogryposis is what they called it at first. In 1981 when John Youngblood was born in Longview, Texas, it was obvious that something was not right about the odd angle of the baby's legs. They were stiff, inflexible. After months of visiting specialists, a new diagnosis came from the doctor at the Scottish Right Hospital in Dallas. He was sure that John John (the name that family and friends would come to call John) was a victim of a congenital spinal defect ("sacral agenesis"). X-rays confirmed that he was born with missing spinal vertebra from the L3 position down and several surgeries would be required as John John grew, to assure that his legs could move, and perhaps make it possible for him to walk.

John John did not know that he was different and began to crawl as most babies do around 6 months of age. At two, following surgery, he learned to walk with small crutches, and by three he could flip his legs into the air and walk on his hands. His father remembers watching the toddler take off like a rocket across the room and how, even then, he exhibited a strong, determined will. Even though he was never without his crutches, John John explored the neighborhood with other kids, climbed trees, and rode his special tricycle fitted for him with hand pedals.

From the 5th grade up, John John had a love for percussion instruments and he began to practice hard on his drums. His dream was to be good enough to one day play in the local junior high band. However, after finally reaching junior high, the director told him he could join the band, but drums were out, because he didn't see how John John would be able to play and march because of his disability. Discouraged but undaunted, John John asked to be transferred to nearby Gilmer High School and the band director there had a different attitude. Not only did he welcome John John to the band, the director devised a way in which he could play the drums (quads) during band perfor-mances. John John stood on the sidelines during the marching routines, then, when the band came forward to perform the special number for the majorettes rou-tine, students were assigned to help carry his drums and a stool onto the field so John John could sit and play with the group. He was elated. He always believed that he could do things others did, if given a chance to do them his way.

His other dream was a little more challenging. When he reached high school, he envied his buddies that went off to football practice. In Texas, football is almost a religion and young men dream of playing the game. John John yearned to be a part of a team as well. One of his band friends was the place kicker for the varsity team and offered to let John John hold the footballs in place while he practiced kicking. So, every day, sometimes even skipping band practice, John John would meet the kicker on the field and they would practice for hours.

Some kids can be vicious and John John endured their cruel taunts and whispers for the most part, but now and then, a sudden anger would rise-up and he would lash out in aggressive ways that got him in trouble at school and then again at home when dad heard about it. But John John refused to see himself as handicapped; he stood up for himself, sending a clear message he would not be pushed around by anyone.

The school hired a new football coach the next year, and at first opportunity, John John showed up on the football field before practice to introduce himself. He approached Head Coach, Mike Mullins and said,

"I'm reporting for practice, Coach."

Puzzled, Coach Mullins looked at him and asked, "What are you going to do?"

Without missing a beat, John John answered, "I am the holder for extra points and field goals."

Coach replied, "Well, okay."

That was that. But, he wasn't assigned a locker, work out gear, a uniform. He was just told to report every day to help the kicker.

He could hardly contain himself when on the very next day he was called with the rest of the team to the cafeteria where he was issued a locker, practice gear, a helmet, shoulder pads and then the clincher; Coach Mullins asked, "What number do you want?"

John John was stunned, "You mean, I'm going to be on the field in a uniform and everything?"

Coach Mullins assured him that was the case and when John John joined the team for team photos that afternoon – it was all the proof he needed. He was indeed a member of the football team, #88 for the Buckeyes of Gilmer High School. It would be two years before John John actually got to play in a real game.

Because of the limited agility in his legs, John John had a unique approach to catching the snaps. He had to sit down flat on his seat, facing the center and take the snap lower to the ground. That posed the possibility of the ball sailing over his head from high snaps. But he kept trying to hone the skill.

He was honored when asked to lead the team out at the start of the first game during his junior year and it was a thrill he never forgot. He continued to lead the team onto the field every game for the next two years and was faithful to show up at practice, while still participating in the band.

Other honors came. John John's senior year was special. For the first time in school history, a student (John John) was named the band President as well as a Team Captain for the football team. However, he knew that time was running out to fulfill his lifelong dream. As football season was drawing to a close, teams were vying for the state playoffs, and there was one game left on the Buckeyes schedule.

As the last game night approached, Coach Mullins began asking John John to take more live snaps in practice. Then, after the pep rally on Friday morning, several students told John John that the local radio station was reporting that a senior boy who uses crutches was going to get to play that night, for Gilmer's last game of the season.

Coach called a team meeting that Friday (without John John), directing everyone else on the team to protect John John and keep him from getting hit, because "This boy is going to play tonight, even if we have to kick a 90 yard field goal!" Later, John John heard that Coach had wanted it all to be a surprise, but it leaked out. It didn't dampen the awesome reality. This was it – the night he would play in a real football game.

I have tried to see these moments through John John's eyes and imagine his emotions. It must have been surreal when in the second half of the game, the Buckeyes scored a touchdown to take the lead and it was time for the field goal try. Coach Mullins suddenly turned to John John and barked,

"Get your butt out there!"

John John excitedly ran out on the field on his crutches then called out the play in the huddle,

"Extra point on center's snap, extra point on center's snap. Ready – break!"

Casting aside his crutches, then turning to sit for the ball, he realized

the kicker is on the sideline having some kind of trouble with his shoe. John John has to call for a time-out. Added seconds caused his heart to pound faster and he shook his nervous hands, but, then it was happening...

Hand raised to call for the ball... the ball hitting his hands hard, almost knocking him over... don't look, just feel the ball, repeat the mantra... laces out, placed right, laces out, placed right... ball is kicked and sails past him... linemen pushing, grunting, making sure John John was not touched... the ball shooting through the uprights... it is up and it is good.

The entire play was only about 2 ½ seconds but for John John it was a 'slow motion' moment that would play over and over, becoming one of his most treasured memories. Looking toward the stands he thought of his dad who only dreamed of having his only son play football. He knew that somewhere in the crowd his dad was proud of him and probably crying like a baby. John John was lifted into the air by his teammates before he could get to his crutches. His "Rudy" moment came that Friday night, and no Super bowl hero has ever been prouder or felt more fulfilled.

John John went on to climb other mountains. He became a valuable member of the local fire department, also was a dispatcher for the Upshur County Sheriff's office. He became connected with a local band and for a time managed them and then came the day when we asked John John to come along with us and manage our merchandise sales. Sometimes I think of him out there selling merchandise, meeting folks town after town, concert after concert. There are certain numbers we do where we invite John John up to play percussion and he's always a hit. Those who are privileged to know John John instantly admire him, and they don't even know his whole story. His father, sent me the following note about his son; it touched my heart,

"Most boys, at least when they are young, look to their dads as heroes. If I look to any living person as heroic, it is my son, John John. God has truly blessed me by allowing me to be his father."

If you ever find yourself close to Gilmer High School, pop in for a look around. You will see a black jersey with the number 88 framed in a huge walnut frame with orange and black borders. Yep, they retired his jersey. There is a picture of John John and the caption underneath reads:

John John Youngblood Team Captain 1997 – 1999

Stand there for a moment and get real quiet. You will be able to hear the roar of the crowd on a special night not so long ago, cheering for a young man who deserves to be everyone's Friday night football hero.

You know, when you think about it, a mountain would be virtually impossible to climb if its surface was completely smooth. There has to be a foothold now and then, an outcropping, a protruding boulder, a tree limb one can grab hold of to pull yourself up. The very things that hinder your

path can actually be used to help you climb. John John has a stubborn tenacity. He doesn't allow his limitations to hinder him from being effective, productive, and a contributor.

Maybe you've noticed them – sometimes climbers will leave markers, a flag, a pile of rocks, or sticks in the ground placed at the top of the mountain as a statement to other climbers. The markers say, "I was here – I conquered this mountain today." John John is respected and admired because he leaves a lot of markers on the mountains every day.

~ Neal

"Today is your day, your mountain is waiting, so get on your way."

—Dr. Suess

"Our way is not soft grass, it's a mountain path with lots of rocks. But it goes upward, forward, toward the sun."

—Ruth Westheimer

NO GOING AROUND THE MOUNTAIN – IT MUST BE CLIMBED

Guy Papa

> *"The beauty of the mountain is hidden for all those who try to discover it from the top, supposing that, one way or an other, one can reach this place directly. The beauty of the mountain is revealed only to those who climbed it ..."*
>
> —*Antoine de Saint-Exupery*

Music is powerful. It can set a mood, move to tears, lift from despair, offer encouragement, help you remember the importance of love, and value what is truly important. The time-worn phrase is true: "music hath powers to sooth the savage breast." I love all types of music, but I am sure one of the reasons I love country music is because the songs usually tell stories from real life. Following is a "real life" story from a fan who loves country music, too. And, (will wonders never cease) he likes our music best!

This special fan is Guy Papa. I met Guy and his family in Rosemont, Illinois when he was eleven years old back in '94. The biggest, happiest grin I have ever seen was on his face. If that joy could be bottled, the world would be changed overnight. I wanted to include Guy's story in the book as a tribute to Guy and his parents. The parents of children with special needs deserve to be honored. From the beginning, the Papas have faced mountains that would terrify the bravest among us. As the title to this chapter suggests, you just can't go around some mountains. My friend, Wayne Newton said it best, "You have to go through the mountains and valleys – because that's what life is: soul growth."

If ever I have met a mom and dad to match the mountain, it is Joe and Karen Papa. They didn't try to find an easier way, they couldn't ignore the mountain, they just strapped on climbing shoes and learned something every day about themselves and what real love and devotion means. They have made it their life purpose to help Guy (and his sister, Jenn) to climb their own mountains, too. No parent can do more.

~ Neal

She was alone in the hospital room when the new mom heard that her new baby, born the day before, had suffered a bleed to the brain. Karen Papa did not really understand what that complication meant. The baby boy, named Guy David was born two and a half months early on August 27, 1982. He was small, only two pounds, 11 ounces, but had been doing fine until this report. Karen would gingerly make the trip down the hospital hall to see her tiny son with tubes and monitors protruding from his fragile little body and it broke her heart.

The doctor explained to Karen and Joe Papa that bleeding to the brain (or intraventricular hemorrhage–IVH) was the condition when bleeding inside or around the ventricles of the brain occurred, which affected the spaces in the brain which contain cerebral spinal fluid. The hemorrhaging is most common in premature babies, especially those with very low birth weight (less than three pounds).

The information was transferred to the parents but the words that registered most with Karen was that she would not be able to hold her baby for three weeks. When she saw him over the next months she would need to get used to the sight of the IV inserted into his head because the strongest veins were in his tiny head. Still he was a beautiful baby and everyone at the hospital began to mention what a fighter the little guy was.

The couple was elated when Guy was finally cleared to go home on November 2nd, two months and five days after his birth. Home was Mundelein, Illinois, located about thirty-five miles northwest of Chicago in northern Lake County. A medium-sized town with good schools and churches, Mundelein is a great place to raise a family. Along with his Italian heritage, Joe Papa owns a strong work ethic and built his life around providing for his family so Karen could remain in the home to care for Guy. Later there would a baby sister as well.

Karen remembers the doctor's words of caution as she left the hospital with her new baby. "No one knows if he will have further health problems, right now, we just need to focus on getting him stronger." Sure enough, Guy began to flourish at home, putting on weight, and already had an infectious smile. Because of the bleed to the brain he was on medication for seizures but seemed to be growing stronger every day.

Their peace was short-lived. During a routine therapy session, the physical therapist told Karen that she suspected Guy had Cerebral Palsy. The young mother nearly crumpled; all she could envision were the children she had seen sitting in wheelchairs, drooling, incapacitated. She was shaken, frightened and despondent and wept the whole way home.

Cerebral palsy was confirmed but the doctor could not tell the Papas the extent of Guy's specific case. Karen knew the news meant the end of their dreams for a perfect child, but then the couple immediately began to create new dreams, new hopes. They would do whatever it took to provide the very best care.

Months passed and there were routine check ups to monitor Guy's status. During one of those neurological exams, when Guy was eighteen months old, came another shocking discovery. The doctor reported that Guy's head was growing faster than normal and a cat scan would be needed. The scan revealed that Guy had hydrocephalus (fluid on the brain) and a shunt would need to be inserted into the brain to drain the spinal fluid into his abdomen.

Karen remembers the fearful hours following surgery. For days Guy just slept, not even taking a bottle. She became totally exhausted from hours on end at the hospital and nearly had to be hospitalized herself. Mother's Day happened to fall during the anxious days and this mother's only wish was for a healthy baby. Karen was elated when the report came that Guy was finally awake and taking a bottle.

Over the years there would be over one hundred shunt revisions and other surgeries for his legs, hips, and eyes. A few days after the little fellow was sent home he acquired a new skill – he spoke his first words and the Papas jokingly add "he hasn't stopped talking since." Whatever limitations Guy had in other areas, his verbal skills would continue to be strong and pronounced.

Guy was nine years old when his sister, Jenn was born. He was delighted with her, entertaining her, spinning her around in her walker. When she cried, he was always alarmed, "Mom, do something – quick!"

It isn't clear exactly when Guy developed a love for music - could have started during an early hospital stay, when Guy's grandmother bought him a wind up pillow which played Brahms Lullaby. The happy melody provided comfort and warmth amid all the hospital noises. The musical pillow also accompanied Guy to his next several surgeries.

Music over the years would continue to give Guy a creative outlet and enjoyment that nothing else would provide. He also would grow to love movies, videos, and listening to the radio. (This is where I come into the picture.) In 1994 I received a request to appear at a benefit concert for a young country DJ, in Rosemont, Illinois who had suddenly died at 28 years of age, leaving a grieving young wife and children. Several other country entertainers joined me for that concert including Dwight Yoakum. Present also at that concert was the Papa family, including eleven year old, Guy. I couldn't escape his smile, it radiated through the entire evening. When I would venture out into the audience as I often do, I would shake Guy's hand and his face would light up and we connected. Later he would beg his mom for one of our CD's. Karen Papa tells me that she knew that Guy was going to be a life long fan, so she gladly purchased the CD and even joined our fan club. I am often privileged to meet our great fan club members back stage and I got to know Guy and his family a little better through these meetings. Turns out that Guy would insist on my CD being played during his many surgeries - other music was just not an option and the doctors and nurses got used to hearing our music in the operating room when Guy was scheduled for surgery.

We enjoy seeing the Papa family at many of our concerts through the years. Whenever we are scheduled near by, or when the Papas can arrange the travel, Guy and family will show up and we always have a good time. I remember a great time at a community cook-out several years ago, hosted by the Papas and their neighbors. Got to visit and had some great homemade fixins,' too!

Then, a special request from an organization called the Starlight Foundation came to us regarding Guy.

This foundation specializes in fulfilling wishes for children with chronic illnesses. Turns out it was Guy's deep desire to record with me and the band. We put our heads together and worked out a plan to fly the family to Nashville so that Guy could record a song with us. A local studio owner donated the studio time and of course, our band provided the background music. We tried to choose a song that we felt would be fairly easy for Guy, but he knew every song I'd ever recorded and could have done any of them. We chose three songs to record with Guy and he was happier than a dog gettin' to ride in the back of a pick up! It was a special joy just to see him enjoying the music. Karen tells me Guy has carried that CD around with him everywhere. He plays it often and is very proud of his musical efforts and rightly so. We were more than happy to provide this great experience for Guy.

The years have passed and Guy is now twenty seven years old. He has been measured with the intelligence and response level of a 2nd or 3rd grader, but his verbal skills are such that he can converse with any adult. In fact he was a DJ for a time at a local radio station, programming all the music for the show as well. Guy chose our songs to play for the most part, so after a while, the radio station personnel asked him to feature other artists too. (I personally see nothing wrong with playing our music exclusively!)

Most days Guy is confined to his wheelchair but can walk with a walker when feeling up to it. Once a week, there are visits from the physical therapist, a tutor, and a caring counselor also meets with Guy. Karen tells me there are some emotional disturbances Guy experiences and the counselor helps Guy through these confusing times.

The debilitating seizures Guy experiences from time to time are a result of the brain shunt and hydro-cephalus. With the seizures come horrific bouts of pain from excruciating headaches. The seizures leave him disoriented; semi-conscious. At times they affect his motor skills and drain him of energy. For days he may be unable to even feed himself. Every day presents challenges that can be frustrating for Guy as well as his family. Still, there is that ever present smile and stalwart effort to perform each task requested of him – tasks that require a great deal of courage and determination.

Guy's sister, Jenn is finishing up her degree at North-ern Kentucky University and Guy loves it when she is home. She is a very loving sister but lives with the con-stant fear that Guy will not be around forever. She has learned as much as anyone to be thankful for each new day. Jenn taught the family dog, Payton, a neat trick. The dog barks out, "I love you" then receives a special treat. The trick delights everyone, especially Guy.

Remember those dreams that Joe and Karen Papa had to recreate for their son, Guy? They remain the same today: that he not suffer; that he live a comfort-able happy life, knowing that he is loved and valued as part of the family; that the life of Guy David Papa be a testimony to true grit and determination; and that

Guy's smile makes someone else's day – every day for many days to come.

There are not many mountains in Northern Illinois where the Papas live. Most of the area is made up of the mega-city of Chicago and surrounding areas. However a little more to the north is Charles Mound, the highest point in Illinois. While looking at the history of the area, I saw that the earliest settler, a farmer, built a house at the base then started cultivating the area in early 1800's. In fact, it became the largest acreage under cultivation in the country around 1835. But, there was this mountain, a huge obstacle that hindered more agricultural pursuits. Finally the farmer, decided to explore the mountain and discovered it produced minerals that would be extremely profitable. The lead and zinc mined from that mountain, the one the farmer thought was going to limit his production initially, made him a rich man.

I can't help believe the same holds true for parents like Joe and Karen Papa. One day they were presented with a mountain – their son's physical limitations. They couldn't go around it – they had to climb it. So they began to pursue what they could learn, achieve, and reap from their experience with Guy that would benefit the family and inspire others. The very mountain that seemed insurmountable, the one that caused them much stress, fear, and endless medical expenses has also made the Papa family wealthy (being rich does not always mean having money). This unique family continues to mine the mountain, and discover veins of riches every day.

The mountain has made them rich in satisfaction – knowing they have provided the best quality of life possible for Guy. They own an enduring patience that produces a certain joy that can't be replicated. The Papas have created a legacy of love – a testament to the deep, everlasting devotion to a son that has inspired countless others. They are also wealthy because they get to witness the presence of a remarkable young man who gets up every day to climb his own mountains.

I can't bark like Payton, Guy, but "I love you, too." See you sometime, somewhere down the road.

~ Neal

SPECIAL THANKS...

I would like to take the time to thank all the folks at Tate Publishing & Enterprises for making the publishing process for my first book such a wonderful experience. From the moment we first started discussing the book right up to the moment it was ready to go to print it has been a truly moving and learning experience for me. The patience they have shown a new author like me is fantastic to see and I'm sure a rarity to find in such a fast paced business. Rita Tate has to be the best creative project manager in the industry. Her advice, support and personal interest has been invaluable. Thanks Mrs. Rita for everything. Let's hope this book is a success, so hopefully we can do it again. Thanks for everything ya'll!

~ Neal McCoy

PHOTOS

Thanks to my road manager, Les Martines for
taking most of the photos we've included.
Appreciate you, Les!

*Neal receiving the prestigious Academy of
Country Music Humanitarian Award*

*Shirley Malone Jackson and her famous
son, NBA great, Karl Malone*

*Neal with Karl Malone at the annual East
Texas Angel Network (ETAN) events*

General Tommy Franks and Neal during Mid East USO tour

Neal entertaining US Soldiers in Kuwait (USO tour)

Neal signing American Flag in Iraq (USO Tour)

Matt Barney in spring of 1994 with Neal in Cerrilos, New Mexico at video shoot for song, Wink. Matt would leave us in 1995

Neal with country music legend Mickey Gilley
along with Al Embry, Branson, 2010

Neal sings the National Anthem at Texas Rangers Baseball game

Neal singing at Wounded Warrior event in Tyler, Texas

Neal with Alan Babin, Branson, Missouri

*Sandy and David Henry took this photo only days before
the tornado of May 3, 1999 that took David's life*

Neal receiving Country Radio Broadcaster's
(CRB) Humanitarian Award

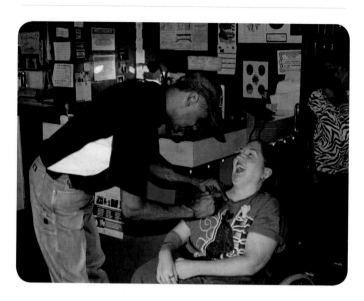

Neal enjoys a laugh with Emily "Butterfly" Snider at ETAN Event

Neal backstage with John John Youngblood

Neal enjoys listening to Guy Papa belt out a song

*Neal and wife Melinda with their
children; MikaAla (Miki) and Swayde*

INFORMATION

For more information about East Texas Angel Network see www.easttexasangelnetwork.com

For Neal McCoy Tour Schedule and special events see www.nealmccoy.com

To order additional copies of
"A New Mountain to Climb"
www.nealmccoy.com
or
www.tatepublishing.com
1-888-361-9473

listen|imagine|view|experience

SONG DOWNLOAD INCLUDED WITH THIS BOOK!

In your hands you hold a complete digital entertainment package. In addition to the paper version, you receive a free download of the song that inspired this book. Simply use the code listed below when visiting our website. Once downloaded to your computer, you can listen to the song through your computer's speakers, burn it to an audio CD or save the file to your portable music device (such as Apple's popular iPod) and listen on the go!

How to get your free song download:

1. Visit www.tatepublishing.com and click on the e|LIVE logo on the home page.
2. Enter the following coupon code:
   6d6a-e13e-b570-d8fd-229d-02bb-4df1-72f0
3. Download the song from your e|LIVE digital locker and begin enjoying your new digital entertainment package today!